Playing Ball on Running Water

Playing Ball

DAVID K. REYNOLDS,
PH.D.

on Running Water

The Japanese Way

to Building a Better Life

QUILL   NEW YORK

Library of Congress Cataloging in Publication Data

Reynolds, David K.
Playing ball on running water.

Bibliography: p.
Includes index.
1. Morita psychotherapy. I. Title.
RC489.M65R5   1984   158'.1   84-8399
ISBN 0-688-03913-8

Printed in the United States of America

BOOK DESIGN BY MARIA EPES

TO MY PARENTS
—who learned life principles by living them

Acknowledgments

Year after year Morita therapists in Japan have patiently explained and enacted their methods for me. Year after year the family of Dr. Hiromu Shimbo has provided my lodging in Tokyo. Year after year my students/patients have offered me their attention and stimulation to develop Morita's ideas in directions useful to the West. This book reflects their investment of effort and commitment, too.

At present ten trainees have been certified to practice Moritist guidance in the United States. The facilities of the ToDo Institute and the Kuroda Institute in Los Angeles and the Health Center Pacific on Maui, Hawaii, have made possible both this intensive training and more general lectures on the subject to wider audiences. During these exchanges, ideas and methods were sharpened to fit Western needs and ways of thinking without, I believe, damage to Morita's insights into the human causes and consequences of neurotic suffering.

From the Moritist perspective, the writing of this book was simply something else that "needed to be done."

Contents

Acknowledgments   7

Part I
Personal Growth Through Morita Guidance   11
Introduction   11
Moving Ahead   15
What It Is That We Teach   17
Meditation, Koans, and Morita Therapy   21
Facing the Inevitable   26
Common Misunderstandings   30
Individual Morita Growth Training   42
Purposeful Living   50
The Mythical Golden Hour   54
Making Mistakes Pay Off   58
Putting Life Off Until Tomorrow   61
Aesthetic Living   65
Trust   67
Heads You Lose, Tails You Lose   70
Talk   72
Gestalt Therapy Parallels   74
Deciding to Decide to Decide   81
Expanding Symptoms   84
Action Prepares   87
Treatment of a Japanese Patient   93

Morita's Life—"Effort *Is* Good Fortune"   97
Student Diaries   99
Exercises in Living—The Ball Game   105
Advanced Exercises   115

Part II
Moritist Fairy Tales and Allegories   117
Introduction   117
The Elevator   118
The Frog Prince   120
Indian Maiden   122
On Trusting   127
Sleeping Sickness   129
Poor Li'l Ugly Ol' Me   130
Aiming Too Low   132
Royalty   135
Stoptime   138
Walls   140
Pain and a Princess   141
A Boy and His Cat   144
The Royal Prisoner   146
The Mouse Who Gave Himself Away   150
Foxes and Feelings   153
Womanikin   156
Snowball   158
A Marvelous Camera   160
Turnabout   163
On Chiming   165
The Coat   168
Summary   171
A Final Note—First Steps   172

Bibliography   174
Index   177

CONTENTS

PERSONAL GROWTH
THROUGH MORITA GUIDANCE

Introduction

There was a time when many mental problems could be cured simply with insight. By understanding the source of the difficulties, by examining their past roots, the patient could find freedom from some sorts of neurotic suffering. Hysterias (such as paralyses with no apparent somatic causes), nightmares, and battle neuroses sometimes responded to the methods of insight therapies. It was almost as if the body/mind complex conspired to force the patient into self-examination. Once that examination was satisfactorily undertaken, there was no longer any need for the symptom.

In a sense, Freud used this method to cure those mental problems not only for his patients, but for the entire Western world. He and his followers put concepts like Oedipus conflict, psychological defenses, superego, repression, psychosexual development, and oral fixation into everyday Western discourse. And with even the rudimentary understanding of their psyches obtained from reading, conversations, and elementary psychology classes, many people found themselves freed from some of their difficulties. Such is the power of insight.

Alas! there are other psychological problems for which psychoanalytic insight offers no cure. Neuroses may be quite subtle these days; they fail to respond to a process of sitting and talking about how we came to be the way we are. They come less from what we have hidden from ourselves than from what we know quite well about ourselves. They come from what we do and don't do as much as from the ways we think and feel. To be cured, these modern forms of suffering require being honest with ourselves not only in thought —but in behavior, as well. Pulling oneself together is a difficult and demanding task in these times. A behavioral commitment is necessary. Insight alone is not enough.

Morita therapy is a character-building process developed in Japan in the early twentieth century. It strengthens those who practice it to surmount problems instead of trying to knock them down. In fact, the word often used in Japanese when doing this therapy is *norikoeru,* which is the same word one would use to indicate climbing over a wall. Isn't that the way many of your problems appear to you? Like walls? Not only the problems created by external circumstances, but also those fears and doubts and worries within. They, too, loom like walls between you and the achievement of the goals you have set for yourself. Yet, it's surprising how low a wall appears when you look back after scaling it. Sometimes the wall disappears entirely. But the strength and skill we develop in going over one wall prepares us for surmounting the next. Granted, some walls in the world we cannot tear down, but we can work hard at becoming better and better at climbing.

This book is about footholds and outcrops you may find useful in scaling some of life's barriers. It also contains exercises to energize your ascent. I wish you the best, but the success of your venture depends on your effort, and yours alone. Yours will be the credit for attaining this new power, yours will be the blame if you merely sit at the foot of the first wall wishing that it were lower.

The serious practice of Morita therapy in the United States began after World War II, when the methods of personal management contained in Morita's thought were found to make experiential sense to Americans as well as to the Japanese. A respectable body of literature on the subject began to appear in English in the 1970's, and formal methods of training and certifying practitioners of the therapy were in operation by 1980.

This book is a sort of progress report on the development of a characteristically Western version of this Eastern therapy, and also a Western interpretation of Morita's understanding of human nature. After all, what Morita wrote in the scientific and medical journals of post–Meiji Japan was the distilled experience of many humans across time. Now we can expand that understanding across cultures, as well. The test of these life suggestions lies in whether they work for all of us. Compare these Eastern notions with your own experience. I think that you will find them useful in a program of personal growth —whether you are a student/patient or a teacher/therapist.

Although Morita was a psychiatrist, physician, and department head of a top medical university in Tokyo, he saw that neurotic suffering is not essentially a medical problem at all—it grows from misunderstandings about life. The solution to neurotic anguish, therefore, is not medical therapy, strictly speaking, but reeducation. This is why we prefer to call those who come to learn how to overcome their unnecessary anxiety and pain students, not patients. In this book, however, I shall refer to such persons variously as clients, students, or patients. But the model to keep in mind is simply that of someone with knowledge and experience in handling discomfort teaching someone else—through conversation, lectures, reading, and exercises of various sorts—how to deal with discomfort.

Neuroses are not illnesses. But, like illnesses, they are painful and they involve suffering. Instead, they are rather unfortunate life-styles that involve hurtful behavior and self-destructive attitudes, and a sort of ignorance about human existence. A medical approach to problems of shyness, unreasonable fears and anxieties, feelings of hopelessness and helplessness, and the like is not necessary—perhaps it is even harmful, plastering over responsibility with a verbal poultice. What is needed is reeducation and practical training in living effectively.

Let me repeat, neurotic people are not ill; they have bad habits of thinking and acting that result in unnecessary suffering for them and for others. In this culture what is offered neurotic people is called psychotherapy. The implication of the word is that there is something "therapeutic" that can be done for the "psyche." No one can heal a mind. All that is necessary is proper reeducation and effort on the part of the student (not patient) to put constructive living principles into daily practice. As an adviser, a personal life-style consultant, and an educator in personal management, strictly speaking, I am neither therapist nor healer. It is the student's efforts that bring about welcome change in his or her life.

Perhaps it would be useful here to say something about the format of this book. In Part I, I have written a series of short, self-contained chapters about Moritist personal growth. These essays provide an introduction to Moritist ideas, which can be supplemented by readings from the bibliography. Part II is a series of original tales and allegories that illustrate various Moritist principles and understandings. Taken together they outline a path of constructive living in a changing world. They point to a way of playing ball on running water.

Moving Ahead

When you awaken at four A.M. and can't go back to sleep, what do you do? When you are angered and frustrated by injustices committed by powerful people in your life, what do you do? Notice that even if you understand the reasons for the sleeplessness or for the anger, the conditions don't go away. Even if you make every effort to will yourself to be sleepy or to be calm, you cannot.

While you are feeling bad, when life isn't turning out as you wish it would, better to accept the insomnia and the anger while directing your efforts toward doing what is useful, productive, and constructive. At four A.M., why not read a magazine or write letters? How about an early-morning walk or shopping at an all-night supermarket? These activities are much more interesting than the inner struggle to conquer insomnia. *It's not fair!* you moan. *Other people sleep through the night!* So you lie there in discomfort, tossing about, now too warm, now too cold, feeling depressed. Then eventually you arise more tired than ever. Life need not include these useless struggles when you learn which parts of yourself to pamper and allow their own way and which parts to control by your own direction.

The other day I was working with my personal computer, trying to get it to print something stored in its memory. I made some entries from the keyboard, but nothing happened. I tried another set of entries; still it didn't work. I tried repeating the process, pushing the keys again and again. How annoying! It ought to work! I found myself pushing harder on the keys in an attempt to exert my will on the computer. But it wasn't programmed to function in that way. The computer didn't care that I was angry and trying to impose my will on it.

Realizing my foolishness, I tried yet another way to get around the obstacle, and this time everything ran smoothly. Fascinating! It was necessary to discover the proper action, then all proceeded in an orderly fashion. No matter how intent and determined I was, no matter how much I desired the result, no matter how emotional or how cool I tried to become, the computer responded only to my actions. Until I did what needed to be done, the results were unsatisfactory.

Like the computer, the world about me responds to my behavior. It can't feel my feelings. Reality doesn't respond to my will or my wishes or my emotions. To believe that positive thinking changes the world directly is childlike naïveté. To be sure, my thoughts and feelings may influence what I do (my behavior), and that action, in turn, may influence reality. But it is what I *do* that affects my world. And it is the same for you.

It follows that if you want to make changes in your marriage or in your job or in your grades at school or in your character, you must change what you are doing. You don't need to change how you feel about something to affect it. For example, if you want closer ties with your spouse, you don't need to begin by loving him or her more. If you want to have more friends, you don't have to begin by feeling less shy or more self-confident. Changes begin with action.

What It Is That We Teach

Morita therapy is overtly a teaching practice. As a guide, I have something to teach my students/clients: namely, a way to live that will relieve unnecessary suffering. It is important to listen to the students' problems and perspectives so that the teaching can be tailored to their needs and explained so that they will be able to understand and be able to try out principles in real experience. There is much to learn in a session. There is no time for the time filler "How do you feel about that?" unless the student is specifically having trouble recognizing and accepting feelings. Complaints and rambling descriptions of emotional ups and downs are discouraged. The goal of Morita therapy is not understanding the distant historical source of our troubling emotions.

Some people believe that when they have some understanding of the childhood origins of their feelings they will have control over them. That impression isn't realistic. We have no control over them unless that knowledge leads to changes of attention and behavior. Insight alone is, for many, a way of avoiding making the effortful, sometimes painful, changes in behavior that are necessary to produce changed feelings and an improved concept of one's self.

Thus it seems reasonable to accept one's feelings as they are (rather than using energy and attention trying to analyze them) and get right to work on attention and behavior. However, such acceptance is not passive; we still work to change our circumstances for the better. We still make efforts to improve the lot of those around us. But the inner turmoil is gone. The conflict within is no more. It is no longer me opposing this condition. It becomes me here doing this. That is all. That is sufficient.

The doing is what is important, not the result. From the Moritist point of view, no act is merely instrumental. Every act is an end in itself. The quality of our attention in action is crucial. Sometimes I work hard and nothing seems to come of the results of the work. I may put in a lot of time weeding, for example, only to find a new crop of weeds springing up within a week. Or a raging forest fire might destroy the cabin that took years to build. However, nothing can take away the changes in my character that resulted from my full attention to that weeding or the building of that cabin. With every fully attended activity I am working not only on the project at hand but on myself as well. Behavior is what counts. Not emotion. Not even the results of behavior. What I do is the only thing in life that I can control. No one can guarantee a life of good feelings. No one can guarantee that our efforts will bring the results that we hope for. We must be clear on what is controllable.

It seems that most folks most of the time simply get through life. Their days are spent merely passing time until the weekends or until their vacations. They mark a few outstanding events—graduation day, the trip to Hawaii, the day they got married, the birth of a child —but the rest of life is unremarkable and meaningless for them. How much richer, it seems to me, to be able to think of every "now" as important, every act as rich with meaning. Such an attitude allows one to *live* life instead of merely enduring it.

In the Moritist context, every act provides the opportunity for purposeful accomplishment and personal growth. Every act can involve moments of directed attention. Pouring a cup of coffee, scrubbing the bathtub, writing a thank-you note, arranging the pages of a photo album, signaling a left turn, setting an alarm, kissing a loved one—all these activities can be, should be, carried out with the clear focus and scrupulous care they deserve. All we have is that flow of attention. If we do not use it with awareness, if we do not recognize its pervasive nature, then we misuse the only treasure we have—we lose life.

DAVID K. REYNOLDS

To be sure, it is *easier* to put out the effort when you come to understand something about yourself, when you have an emotional high, when you enjoy the meal I cooked, when you choose life rather than self-destruction. But *I* never cause these choices and experiences for you. I never control them. I never control you. My responsibility, my control, lies only in the sphere of my own behavior. What results is up to you and reality. Being in charge of me is a full-time job.

Responsibility is an important topic for consideration here. It is critical to distinguish between understanding and condoning. The former has nothing to do with responsibility; the latter assigns it elsewhere. Western psychotherapy, in its attempt to understand disturbed behavior, bends over backward and ends up condoning or excusing hurtful, destructive acts. Look at all the extenuating psychological circumstances that affect our criminal justice system's decisions. In Morita therapy we are quite clear on the boundary between understanding and condoning. We seek to understand and condone any feeling, any feeling at all. The desire to kill or steal, fear, shyness, panic, sexual attraction, disgust, pride, joy, reverence, and so forth are all equally acceptable, that is, to be accepted as they are. There is nothing wrong with any of these feelings. They are not acts. They may cause us discomfort, but they don't directly affect anyone else.

On the other hand, we seek to understand, but refuse to condone, any harmful behavior, no matter what the confused and powerful feelings that lie behind them. Behavior or acts are the only ways we directly affect other people. To feel like killing another human is natural in some circumstances; to actually kill another human is wrong. I may want to understand what is going through the mind of a murderer before the crime, but, whatever he is thinking or feeling, the murder cannot be condoned. It is quite a relief, actually, when we realize that we have no responsibility for our feelings. They are uncontrollable; they are natural; they need only be accepted as they are. Still, we must take clear responsibility for what we do, and we must hold others responsible for what they do. If we fail to do so, we run the risk of just the sorts of injustices that appear in the name of justice in our courts every day.

When the courts punish (fine) parents for a crime committed by their children, the reason for the punishment should not be that they are responsible for their children's behavior. They are not. Each of us is responsible for his or her own behavior, even children. The punishment is justified because of the parents' improper parenting—their behavior was at fault and not their lack of control over their children's behavior. Can you see how important the difference is? To hold one of us responsible for another's behavior is meaningless for the one and demeaning for the other. I simply cannot control what you do. You cannot be absolved of responsibility for what you do. It is as simple as that.

Meditation, Koans, and Morita Therapy

Meditation is a sort of focused attention. The process of meditation involves returning one's attention again and again to that focus. The focus may be counting one's breaths, or a mantra (incantation), or an image, a prayer, a Zen koan (puzzle), body sensations, or almost anything. Attention drifts to other topics and is redirected to the object of attention again and again. A good description of this channeling of attention may be found in Philip Kapleau's book, *The Three Pillars of Zen: Teaching, Practice, Enlightenment.* That book deals with Zen meditation, but the principle of disciplining attention is common to all meditative forms.

Occasionally, I assign quiet-sitting meditation to a client. Quiet-sitting meditation is simply sitting in some comfortable position that doesn't interfere with breathing and doesn't require considerable shifting around for about thirty minutes at a time. The focus of attention is ordinarily the breathing, either counting breaths or mentally "observing" the flow of air into and out of the lungs. As described above, the mind drifts, stray thoughts pass through, and attention is returned again and again to the breathing. This exercise is to be carried out daily once or twice for a half hour each time.

Quiet-sitting meditation (for further information, see the chapter on *seiza* in my *The Quiet Therapies*) is particularly helpful for people who use their minds to escape from the problems that reality has brought them. Such people develop the pattern of letting their minds flit from topic to topic in endless shallow mental activity. These people may be alternately called dingy, flaky, distractable, or hyperactive, but they share the characteristic of trying to avoid facing reality by refusing to allow their minds to settle long on any subject. Thus, their strategy to avoid suffering is to avoid thoughts that might cause it. Jokes, puns, quick shifts in conversation, physical movement from place to place, changes in dress and decor sometimes mark the desperate attempts to avoid reality in these bright but immature people.

Quiet sitting forces their bodies to be still for longer than their nervous activity ordinarily allows. As is typical of Morita's approach, we begin by changing behavior—with resultant changes in thought and mood. Stilling the body in time forces the mind to cease its panicky attempt to flee endlessly. The anguish of confronting past failures and future dilemmas washes over the meditator. There is pain, but also strengthening. One doesn't die passing through this gate, though the passage is filled with hurt. For some people, it is a necessary prerequisite for full attention to daily living.

I think of quiet-sitting assignments rather like hospitalization. Both are specialized treatments for particular sorts of problems. We don't hospitalize people in Morita therapy facilities in Japan unless the patient is already staying home from work or school. Those who are so disturbed that they cannot do their work or study need to be removed to a sheltered setting where they can be reeducated toward more constructive living. On the other hand, if the patient is (however painfully) working or attending classes, there is ordinarily no need for hospitalization. Why withdraw a person from his everyday reality in order to teach him to live well in everyday reality? Much better seems to be the plan of providing outpatient and group support while the suffering person continues with his daily activities in his "ordinary" surroundings.

It is the same with silent self-reflection. The daily practice of Morita's method is meditation in itself. The focus of attention is brought back again and again to what reality has brought us in each moment. The themes of knowing our purpose, accepting our feelings, and doing what needs to be done are scanned again and again throughout the day. Attention wanders; reality reminds us that our

DAVID K. REYNOLDS

mindfulness has slipped; again we return to awareness of our immediate circumstances. For those who can practice this form of walking, everyday meditation, there is no need to assign quiet-sitting meditation (though the individual may decide for himself or herself that such sitting is something that needs to be done).

I must be clear here that I refer to meditation as a therapeutic tool to achieve a certain stilling of the mind in order to allow subsequent attention to moving about in ordinary life. I am not referring to meditative practices, such as zazen, a Buddhist form of sitting meditation, which aim at religious or extraordinary experience. The purposes are different, at least in degree. I have no idea what "enlightenment" might be. At this level I am concerned with tasting my food, driving my car, and putting the key in the lock with full attention.

Occasionally, we use Zen koans in the practice of Morita therapy in the United States. Again, the way in which we use them and the purpose for employing them is somewhat different from those of Zen Buddhism. A koan is a sort of puzzle with a solution that must be arrived at by more than rational thought. Like a good chess problem, a koan has one proper solution, and when one has discovered it, there is a certainty that needs no confirmation from another, though it might be helpful to consult with an expert to ensure that nothing has been overlooked. But unlike a chess problem, the koan's solution is beyond logic.

Some of the koans we modify for use in Morita therapy are listed below:

1. Doshin: "Open the gate of release for me!"
   Sosan: "Who has constrained you?"
   Doshin: "No one constrains me."
   Sosan: "Then why do you ask for release?"
2. Hyakujo said to his monks, "There's a man who eats sparingly, but is never hungry; there's a man who is always eating, and never full."
3. Somebody comes into the Zen Center with a lighted cigarette, walks up to the Buddha statue, blows smoke in its face, and drops ashes on its lap. You are standing there. What can you do?

4. Likuko said to Nansen, "In my house there is a stone that sits up or lies down. I intend to carve it as a Buddha. Can I do it?" Nansen answered, "Yes, you can."
Likuko persisted, "Can I really do it?"
Nansen answered, "No, you cannot!"
5. A monk asked Funyo, "If there is not a cloud in the sky for ten thousand miles, what would you say about that?"
"I would punish the sky with my stick," Funyo replied.
"Why blame the sky?" the monk persisted.
"Because," Funyo answered, "there is no rain when we need it and no fair weather when we should have it."
6. A monk told Joshu, "I have just entered the monastery. Please teach me."
Joshu asked, "Have you eaten?"
The monk replied, "Yes, I have eaten."
Joshu said, "Then you had better wash your bowl."
7. Dogo said, "It is like a man feeling for the pillow at his back at midnight."
Ungan said, "I have got it."
Dogo asked, "How have you got it?"
Ungan said, "The whole body is the eye and the hand."
8. A monk asked Master Tozan, "How can one escape from winter cold and summer heat?" Tozan said, "Why do you not go to a place where there is neither cold nor heat?"
The monk said, "What is the place without cold, without heat?" Tozan said, "When it is cold, the cold freezes you. When it is hot, the heat burns you."
9. A monk asked master Sozan, "The snow covers a thousand hills, but why is only the one peak not white?"
Sozan said, "You should know the absurdity of absurdities."
The monk asked, "What is the absurdity of absurdities?"
Sozan said, "Being of a different color from the rest of the hills."
10. The monkey is reaching for the moon in the water,
Until death overtakes him he'll never give up.
If he'd let go the branch and disappear in the deep pool,
The whole world would shine with dazzling pureness.

DAVID K. REYNOLDS

Of course, it would not be appropriate to give the answers to the koans here, but I can offer some hints about the true subject matter of the koans from the Moritist perspective. The first two have to do with the subjective nature of neurosis (suffering); the third tests the student's level of understanding about what needs to be done in a given situation; the fourth asks the student to recognize the stone and to discover why the master's sudden change of mind came about. The next is about possibilities; the sixth is about practicalities; and the seventh is about perspectives; the eighth koan is about acceptance; the ninth is about the absurdity of uniqueness; and the last describes a strange misunderstanding. They all teach us about ourselves if we are willing and prepared to learn from them.

Facing the Inevitable

Writing your obituary, epitaph, and eulogy can be a revealing experience. I've done it several times and find it a useful assignment for many of the people with whom I work. The three fundamental principles of the Moritist method of personal management are to accept your feelings, know your purpose, and do what needs doing. The exercise of writing an obituary, epitaph, and eulogy helps us to examine our long-term purposes, our life goals, what needs doing. It is really not so much a way of dealing with our inevitable deaths as it is a way of ordering our lives until then.

Your obituary is the notice that will appear in your local newspaper once you have died. It provides your age and lists your survivors; it may contain your occupation, the cause of death, time and place of services, and your memorable accomplishments. Project your imagination into the future. Where will you be? How are you likely to die? Who will survive you at that time? What will you have accomplished by then? Consider this future event and write a realistic obituary for yourself.

Your epitaph is the pithy sentence or phrase carved on your tombstone. It is the brief summation of your life—the condensation, in words, of your whole being. What memorable statement do you want to leave to the world on your tombstone or memorial tablet? How do you wish to be remembered? To whom will this statement be addressed?

Your eulogy is the longer statement that one or more persons will present publicly at your funeral or memorial service. What will they say about you? Here you can give freer rein to your expectations about the future. Look at the details of where you will live, what sorts of work you will do, with whom you will be living, your temperament, your favorite foods and reading materials, your financial situation, your philosophical and religious beliefs, your health, and so forth from birth until death.

Now consider for a moment what isn't contained in these documents. What would you have liked to do with your life but didn't? What tasks remained unfinished when you died? What tasks remained unbegun? What was not in your history that could have been with some effort on your part? Which people? Which successes? Which skills? Which travel experiences? Look for the blanks and evaluate what you must do now to begin to fill them before you die.

You may find this exercise depressing; looking at one's prospective death is an unpleasant undertaking for many people. Furthermore, finding that little has been accomplished in one's life may precipitate bitterness and disappointment. But, whatever feelings emerge, you have faced these existential issues—a necessary undertaking. What you do in the years ahead is important. What you are doing right now is even more important. Now is the only time you will ever be given to begin changes that will result in your being at the place where you want to be when you die. What needs to be done? Do it.

We are all going to die. It is important to restimulate awareness of this basic truth over and over. There are a number of characteristic ways of dealing with death; we all use most of them at one time or another. One method is to try to delay it as long as possible—for example, by wearing seat belts, following a health regimen, obtaining proper medical care, and avoiding dangerous situations. Ignoring death—resigning oneself to its inevitability and "forgetting" about it —is another way of dealing with our mortality.

A third strategy is to "grab for all the gusto" of life. "You only go 'round once in this life." Death becomes a marker, a motivator for living one's limited time fully, and an excuse for self-indulgence. Death also can be reinterpreted intellectually and thus trivialized.

There is much talk these days of death being a "natural end point" to life. Philosophically, death is seen as a normal element in nature's evolutionary process, necessary for the survival of the new and for the initiation of variety and change. The awesomeness of one's own death is thus minimized from this distant perspective.

Some people compete with death. They tempt it with life-risking activities. Others work hard to win a few points in life before losing the game; they seek to leave their mark on the world before their final play is made. Others distance themselves from death artistically or with social rituals. For example, the Days of the Dead are celebrated in parts of Mexico. Candies are made in the shape of skulls, skeleton puppets dance, paintings with death themes are displayed, songs about death are sung.

Some seek immortality through disciplines or arcane knowledge, faith or social contribution, or some other means. And many hedge their bets by adopting more than one of these methods.

Despite our every effort, we still retain an innate fear of personal death. Gregory Zilboorg wrote that there "always lurks the basic fear of death." Ernest Becker, in *The Denial of Death,* argued that no one is immune from this fear. Morita, too, pointed out this dread of the end point of life. Characteristically, Morita pointed out its usefulness to the individual and to the species. Unpleasant though it may be to cringe before the notion of termination, this fear prompts not only acts of self-preservation but also self-development and personal achievement. In the early years of the twentieth century Morita had already seen the one-dimensional relationship between self-protection and actualization. It is not only that we desire to live, but that we desire to live fully, to live well, to live to our maximum capacity. Furthermore, we resist with great energy and determination anything that stands in the way of this living of life to its fullest.

Sometimes such barriers are within ourselves. We struggle with our own emotions and habits of behavior in an attempt to push away the deathlike grip of limited living. That struggle is the main reason for your reading this book. In these writings you find information to help you direct your efforts effectively.

Viktor Frankl, in *Man's Search for Meaning,* wrote of tucking our deeds safely into the calendar of the past. I want much the same thing

DAVID K. REYNOLDS

for my students and clients. That is, a year from now they should be able to look back and see how much they did that needed doing in this year—not how much turned out well, or even how much was finally accomplished. It is the quality of the doing in which we take pride. Again, "take pride" isn't the same as "feeling pride" or being boastful about a deed. Taking pride in something is a quality of the act and not a quality of mine as I look back on it. The experience is something akin to watching a professional football player or a symphony conductor—I can respect and admire what they do, even "take pride in it," without claiming credit for their work. The I of the past is someone akin to me, and I care about his historical doing, but he is not me, now.

An intelligent but very quiet member of one of the Morita guidance groups told me that he held back the words that came to his mind because he didn't know whether they would be helpful to others in the group. The other participants seemed to be offering helpful support and advice, and he wasn't certain whether his contribution would be up to par. So he sat silently until I prodded him into participation.

In our individual counseling session, I advised him to offer his words to the group as a gift. He need not determine beforehand whether they will be helpful or not. If they are presented with this gift-giving attitude, he can leave it up to the other group members what they will do with his present. They may accept and use his gift as they see fit. He has no responsibility for what others do with his offering; all that he need do is offer it.

Common Misunderstandings

As Morita's ideas are presented to Western audiences through lectures and books and individual training, there are certain problem areas or misconceptions that arise with some regularity. These troublesome points are rooted in characteristically Western ways of viewing life, the mind, freedom, and other aspects of human existence. It is not that these Western attitudes are wrong, but that there are other perspectives that are useful too. We don't want to close our minds to possibilities that might prove helpful in our everyday living. I must emphasize again that the Morita lifeway doesn't ask for belief or commitment or joining a group; it recommends only an open mind. Compare these writings with your own experience, not with the way you wish things were or with the way you were taught things ought to be. I know that you will find a lot of practical human wisdom in these ideas. They will help you clarify problems in your own life and, what's more, they will provide sound methods for dealing with these problems. Give it a try and see the results.

One young woman was feeling guilty about wanting to change her husband's drinking and smoking habits. She asked herself, Don't we emphasize in Morita therapy that we cannot control other people? That our responsibility is for our own behavior? The behavior of others may be unpleasant to us and harmful to themselves, but don't we have to accept their behavior as it is (just as we accept feelings as they are) without attempting to control the uncontrollable? she wondered. So when she began to refuse to buy beer for her husband on her shopping trips, he said nothing, but she felt guilty about her efforts to influence his drinking.

Her misunderstanding was in confusing effort with results. There is nothing wrong with trying to influence others. We do it all the time. This book is my attempt to influence the way you think about certain things, and to influence what you do. Almost everything we say is an effort to influence others, at the very least to influence them to listen to us. Trying to affect other people is a natural, everyday aspect of human life. There is nothing inherently wrong with it, however concealing these efforts, using physical force, or using our influence to obtain certain goals may be wrong in many circumstances. On the other hand, to be attached to or to be obsessed with the effects of our actions to influence others is a mistake. Like any behavior, actions to change another person should be undertaken with full attention and wholeheartedly. But then we must leave it up to the person to decide whether to change or not.

I am indifferent to whether you understand and accept the life principles in this book. Some of you will find them intriguing and immediately beneficial. Others will reject them out of hand. That is your business. My success or failure lies not in whether I have convinced you of the wisdom of Morita's method, but in the quality of my presentation. If I have written with full attention, as well as I can, then the outcome is of interest to me but not crucially important.

It is the same thing for the young housewife. She is quite appropriately concerned with her husband's problem. Smoking and excessive drinking are very likely to shorten his life. She has every right to attempt to influence his habits. She has been quite clear with him about her purposes. But there her attachment must stop. Whether he stops drinking and smoking is his concern. She is personally interested in the outcome of her efforts, but she must not judge them in terms of the outcome. She does need to know if he stops in order to know whether she needs to continue trying to influence him to quit. But she must leave up to her husband, and him alone, the decision about how to respond to her behavior.

She cannot control him; she must not commit herself to controlling him. But, for her part, she is responsible for doing what she can to achieve her purpose. Again, her purpose is not to control him; her purpose is influencing, not the resultant effect. Is this crucial difference clear to you? We have defined her purpose in terms of something that she can control—it is a game she can win and need not feel guilty about. (Of course, she may continue to feel guilty, in which case she must accept her guilt feelings and keep on doing what she has determined to do.) By focusing on the *influencing* she is dealing with the possible.

Stan complains that he feels small and weak when he goes to the bank. He is unshaven, unkempt. There are blotches of oil on his work pants and shirt, and therefore he thinks the tellers despise him. Stan, at first, tries to ignore his intuitions. He wants to deny his feelings of discomfort in the presence of their disdainful stares. But he really does feel terrible. Doesn't Morita therapy offer a way to get rid of these feelings? Doesn't it offer peace of mind?

First of all, Stan must learn that trying to escape from his discomfort is what this method is *not* about. He feels demeaned by the tellers' attitude. He also feels inappropriately dressed for doing bank business. Perhaps what needs to be done is to shave and wash and comb his hair and dress in cleaner clothes. Perhaps what needs to be done is to speak to the teller about his discomfort. Or to apologize. Or to find another bank. Or to keep on with circumstances as they are but to focus more on getting the bank transaction accomplished despite his discomfort. It is up to Stan to decide what needs doing.

Nevertheless, Stan must never attempt to hide away or suppress his emotions. They should never be ignored or denied. They provide important information about what needs to be done. They are worthy of being felt even when they are painful. Probably, they will fade over time unless Stan does something to restimulate them. But, they must be accepted while Stan gets on with the business of doing what the situation of the moment requires him to do. It is characteristic of Stan that, when I asked him if he had completed his bank business in spite of his feelings, he was surprised to be able to answer that he had. He'd been so tied up in his worries about what the tellers were thinking of him that he hadn't noticed that he'd accomplished his banking. Stan is still feeling-centered and not yet purpose-centered. As his focus changes, he will begin to notice his successes in action, and he will be less swayed by the fruitless attempt to feel comfortable and at peace all of the time.

Laurel's perfectionistic planning interferes with her active participation in reality. She reasons this way: I want a job, but first I should prepare thoroughly for finding a job. In order to prepare I must seek out all relevant information about jobs. But I can't search for information with maximum efficiency while suffering this way. So I really should straighten out my life first. In order to straighten out my life I should undergo some psychotherapy. Now in order to select the best psychotherapy I should get lots of information about therapies. To use that information about therapies most effectively (that is, to make the wisest decision about which therapy to undergo) I should be in top mental condition. But I'm not in top mental condition, so it follows that I can't do any of these things. Most of all, I'm in no condition to look for a job.

This is the sort of logical but unrealistic thinking by which some neurotic persons separate themselves from their original purposes—in Laurel's case, to find a job. It is better for her to begin the search for work even without absolutely thorough preparation and without confidence. The difficulties she encounters in the real pursuit of work will teach her more than mental wheel spinning. In Morita therapy we don't invest time in pondering why the client is involved in this or that self-defeating game. To play the game of exploring the depths of the psyche is simply to participate in the same wheel spinning that is the problem—it is of the nature, "I must understand and straighten out my psyche before I can go on about finding the job or otherwise participate in life."

Laurel and I explored the manner in which one looks for work, and I encouraged Laurel to straightforwardly begin looking. It may turn out that finding work is not what needs to be done, after all. But that discovery is most readily made while Laurel is engaged in job hunting, not while lying on a couch. We do what we set out to do until there is something more important that needs to be done. Then, without regret or broken stride, we turn wholeheartedly to the next endeavor.

Do not misunderstand. There is room for reflection and planning within the Moritist method. But those who come for our training are prone to overplanning and underacting; they feel and think a great deal and do very little. What needs to be done often is to sit and map out a plan of action. My students often need to be prodded to find out about reality by acting on and in it.

Scott needs a new place to live. The apartments of Scott's choice are in the area near my office, so we decide to use the therapy hour to go looking for an apartment. There is nothing magical or even necessary about doing therapy in an office. Morita therapy concerns everyday living. It is not confined to one particular setting. Therefore, it is appropriate to leave the office and to go walking with Scott in his search for a place to live. As we walk, Scott begins his usual monologue of troubles. His brothers don't care for him; there is a financial crisis at work; relationships with women are going sour. I ask him what the street numbers are on this block. What was the color of the car that we just passed? For a moment Scott wonders if I am so coldhearted that I'm not at all concerned with his problems. Then he realizes that reciting his woes again and again is not helping at all; furthermore, during the recitation he misses what is happening right now.

Scott assumed I would find the apartment building for him. I didn't. Scott thought that I would console him. I didn't. It isn't that a Morita therapist doesn't care what is troubling his student/client. Rather, I care so much that I must do what I can to make Scott do what he needs to do in the moment. Scott gets so lost in the difficulties of the past week that he forgets his key when he leaves his room. He is so distracted by worry that he doesn't notice what reality is bringing him *right now.* I can't let Scott follow me to his apartment building. He must get there on his own. I'll go *with* him as an indication of support.

Most of my Western students need to be reminded that acceptance does not equal passivity. In the West we are taught that the first step in controlling something is to understand it, then to act on it to make it change. Of course, we run into all sorts of difficulties with this approach whenever we encounter something that cannot be understood rationally—death, for example, and emotions (such as love and despair) and the sacred. We aren't taught the usefulness of accepting reality, both that part of it we can change and that part we can't. We may see acceptance as a sort of giving up, a last resort. In fact, acceptance of the way things are is always the first step in changing things. Denial of reality, resistance to reality, fantasies, and even elaborate plans don't accomplish change.

One young woman saw herself as the passive victim of fate. Her strategy of living was to be as harmless as possible and hope that others would recognize her "niceness" and take care of her. When asked what she would do if someone dropped ashes on her precious statue of the Buddha, she replied that she wouldn't do anything. Perhaps she thought that inactivity was the equivalent of accepting reality. But, passivity is far from my mind when I speak of acceptance.

When someone drops ashes on my Buddha, that reality must be accepted, but there is something that I need to do. Do you remember the koan about dropping the ashes on the Buddha? It is the third in the list of koans presented on page 23. It represents our reaction to anyone who, through ignorance or through malice, soils something that is precious to us: a rape, an undeserved job loss, a divorce, a rumor, all may represent the dropping of ashes on our Buddhas. In these cases we must distinguish between positive acceptance and negative passivity. One of the assignments given the young woman in question was to reflect upon the ways in which she is "one-who-destroys." That is, she has killed others' dreams, she has killed their time and her own, she has wasted her parents' money, and so forth. It was very difficult for her to begin to see the ways in which she is also an active agent of harm in everyday life and not solely a victim.

Another misconception is closely related to the last. It has to do with words like *I can't* or *I don't seem to be willing to* or *It appears that I'm unable to.* I can't help but smile as I remember an evening in one of our drop-in Morita therapy groups. A slim black woman in her early thirties was sitting directly across from me in the circle. She was a former Morita student/client whom I hadn't seen for nearly a year.

"How is work going these days?" I asked.

"Oh, just fine," she replied.

"Are you driving to work every day?"

"Sure." She looked as if she were wondering why I had asked that question. Of course she was driving to work every day. Doesn't everyone? Then a big smile broke across her face. She explained to the group that a little over a year before just getting out of her house was a major and terrifying undertaking. And driving her car to work was a traumatic episode. She could take only one route to work. Even that route was frightening, but at least it was familiar, with a minimum number of left turns. How she struggled with herself each morning! How she doubted her ability to stick out her new job! Yet, now, only a little more than a year later, driving was so natural to her that my question had sounded odd. Of course she drove to work!

"I can't" can mean that it is physically impossible to do something ("I can't be twelve feet tall," "I can't leap ten yards") or it can mean that I doubt my ability to do something that is possible ("I can't talk with the professor about the grade on this exam," "I can't ask him to lunch"). We evaluate our ability to do something on the basis of whether we have, in fact, done it in the past. Once we do it, the issue of can/cannot need not arise under similar circumstances later. Of course, some people use "I can't" to mean "I don't want to" or "I am afraid to" or "I have no confidence in my ability to" or something of the sort. The surest way of discovering the limits of our abilities is to act. Reality will demonstrate to us what we can do and what we cannot.

The great majority of people who come to me for training have used "I can't" so loosely that they have limited themselves unnecessarily. To say the opposite, "I can," is no different, really. When you get down to it, the action will tell the tale. Acting on reality gets us some response from reality. And it is that response that tells us about ourselves in the world. We learn our true capabilities, our true limitations, and, invariably, what needs to be done next.

DAVID K. REYNOLDS

The concept of freedom is another stumbling block for some Western patients. From the Moritist point of view, we are most free when we have the greatest skill at living life, that is, when we are self-disciplined. Skilled painters practice to master basic technique, then they are free to improvise. They also recognize the limits of the medium with which they work. They are responsible, that is, "respondible," to their medium. They work with the situation (including the materials) at hand. Freedom is possible only when limits are recognized, self-disciplined skills are developed, and the immediate circumstance is utilized with full attention. Some Westerners seem to think of freedom as an amorphous state beyond limits, beyond discipline, beyond circumstances. Such impulsive, random, irresponsible behavior is not characteristic of freedom but of immaturity and meaninglessness. This artificial freedom is not worth the investment of our thought and action.

Some people seem to have trouble with the important distinction between intellectual and experiential understanding. The other night in one of our groups a young woman was talking about seeking a mate. The way she was going about finding an acceptable male was to sit at home refining her vision of what sort of fellow he should be. She said that she wanted to specify clearly in her mind just what this ideal type would be like so that she wouldn't have any regrets when she found someone who fit the mold and was worthy of her total commitment. I suggested that a better strategy might be to go out with a variety of men until she came across one she found worthy of getting to know better. She wanted to imagine and plan; I wanted her to act.

Kim, let's call her, is a typical *shinkeishitsu* type of person. She wants to figure everything out beforehand. She overplans and underacts. She goes unemployed for months as she considers what would be the ideal job. She immobilizes herself with her intellect. Getting up in the morning requires a long, involved working out of the theoretical necessity of getting up. In my experience, events very rarely turn out as I expected them to when I had nervously rehearsed them over and over in my mind. The most effective way to find out what is going to happen is to live through the event. Of course, there are limits to this approach. I'm not suggesting that planning and predicting likely outcomes are never appropriate. But for a lot of people, like Kim, there is too much mental wheel spinning and not enough experiencing reality through action.

Kim can justify her careful planning with a clearly presented argument. But behind her search for precision is a fear of the muddied, complex reality. Her thoughts are "safer" than risking a date. Because she resists accumulating knowledge through experience (as opposed to intellect), she finds herself with little experiential knowledge upon which to base her idealistic planning. That lack of experience, and the confidence that comes from knowing through experience, makes Kim even more afraid of testing reality through behavior. She needs to act and then, succeed or fail, she needs to act some more. Her experiential understanding of reality will help her to trust her actions. By trust I don't mean that she will like doing them, necessarily. But reality can be trusted to give feedback on courses of action. Out of a hundred possible outcomes of applying for a particular job (and Kim can imagine most of them), reality will send her only one. Kim will learn more useful information from that single real result than from days of anticipating possibilities.

With students/clients like Kim I emphasize the simplicity of action. She either does or doesn't do her therapy assignment for the week. Such statements as "I decided to do it," "I tried to do it," "I wanted to do it," "I intended to do it," "I would have done it, except . . ." add nothing to the reality that it was or was not accomplished. Kim would relish a complicated discussion about the conflicting motivations that led her to skip her weekly assignment. She doesn't need to *decide* to write in her journal, I remind her, she just needs to write.

The way we usually figure out that we decided to do something is to look back and see if we did it. If we did it, we must have decided to do it. "I tried to" may mean simply that we started doing some task, then did something else. All the talk about intention and motivation can be a smoke screen we throw up to justify what we, in fact, did. I won't let Kim play these sophisticated psychological games during our sessions together. Instead, I ask her what she did. That

DAVID K. REYNOLDS

action is reality. That action produced experience. That action is the basis for vital experiential knowledge.

Tim lies in bed until after noon nearly every day. In that way he can avoid meeting people during the morning. He says he does this because he feels lazy. I tell him that he feels lazy because he lies in bed all morning.

Tim goes on to complain that "people around me don't support me. That's why I'm in the shape I'm in now." Yet it is Tim who decides what Tim does. Better yet, Tim does what Tim does, not the people around him. It is pleasant to feel supported. It is difficult to do what needs to be done when we don't feel supported. It is difficult —but necessary.

"I'll *try* to do what is on this list," Tim says.

"It isn't necessary to try," I tell him. "Just do what is on that list."

It isn't necessary to want to or to decide to or to get it together in order to or to motivate oneself to or make the effort to or otherwise insert some step before the doing. It is the doing that counts.

People have all sorts of mistaken notions about failure. An acquaintance of mine arrived at work thirty minutes late because of rainy weather that slowed her bus. All the while she sat on the bus, her mind was filled with thoughts about being late. Perhaps she should quit after behaving so irresponsibly. Would she be scolded by her employer? Couldn't the bus go any faster? How could she explain her tardiness satisfactorily?

Her failure was not in arriving late for work (a condition outside of her reasonable control), but in "losing" the hour she sat worrying on the bus. That time could have been spent observing her surroundings, reading a magazine, writing a letter, planning a vacation.

Earlier this year in Tokyo I caught the wrong local train while talking with a friend. We rode for five or six stops deeply engrossed in our conversation before we realized our mistake. Hurriedly, we exited from the train and stood on the platform. My friend was feeling very foolish. He scratched his head and smiled at our error.

For a moment I thought, *How interesting, this thing that has happened.* Then my mind immediately turned to what needed to be done next. I began looking around for the platform that would take us back along the way we had come. There was no time for lengthy self-criticism and internally berating myself for being stupid and inattentive. Whether we've arrived at our intended destination or not, reality signals us something that needs to be done right now. It is the quality of noting what reality presents to us and acting forthrightly that I wish to pass along to my students.

Darlene sees life as a single game at which she succeeds or fails. Her assessment of life soars at times when she considers herself a success, and it plunges when she thinks of herself as a failure. In her eyes, she is either total victor or absolute vanquished, perfectly good or perfectly awful, on top of the world or a doormat. A single event can swing her self-evaluation completely around. One failure and she is a total flop, hating herself, only burdening others by living.

Yet life is so much richer than Darlene's view allows. It presents thousands and thousands of mini-successes and mini-failures each day, if one wants to look at them as such. Life presents moment-by-moment challenges, cues about the adequacy of our responses to them, and then—immediately—new challenges. There is no need to try to select out and analyze this myriad of choice/act/feeling events, no need to summarize them into a global self-evaluation. There is no time to do so as new events push forward into our attention, requiring immediate appropriate responses.

When Darlene comes to see more of what life is bringing her now and now and now, she will move beyond the roller-coaster concept of self she now has.

Recently, I spoke before a group of psychotherapists. They had the usual difficulty with the notion that a neurotic symptom is only a problem when we are noticing it. In this particular group the discussion centered around rage. Some psychoanalytically oriented therapists wanted to know what we in Morita therapy do about the rage the clients may feel toward their parents. I pointed out that clients must do the same thing with rage that they must do with any feeling when it appears: that is, to accept it and go on about doing what needs doing. "But what about the rage that is bottled up?" they asked. "Bottled up where?" I wanted to know.

There is no "hidden" rage. Where would we hide it? When we are angry at our parents, we are angry at them. Why do we need to assume that such anger lingers around somewhere in our psyches outside of our awareness? In Morita therapy, all we work with is the flow of awareness that is me in this moment. That is all we ever have to work with. When this me-now is filled with self-conscious shyness, which interferes with my speaking to a group, then shyness is a problem for that me-now. I need a strategy for dealing with that problem now. But when I am deeply involved in a discussion about Japanese character, and no self-conscious shyness intrudes at that moment, then there is no need to assume that the shyness is lurking around somewhere waiting to emerge. I am never entirely assertive nor entirely shy, neither clever nor stupid, neither neurotic nor healthy. I am sometimes this, sometimes that. I am a constantly changing flow of awareness. I am only me-now.

You see, the notion that a symptom is still "there," somehow, even when we don't notice it, is tied to the notion that we have only a single personality. When you believe that you are sadistic or authoritarian or kind or sensitive or schizophrenic or odd or bright or loving, then you have to figure out something to explain why you are sometimes out of character. If you see yourself as an angry person and, yet, sometimes you are gentle and loving, then you have to believe that the anger is still there somewhere (repressed, perhaps) to preserve your image of yourself as angry. It isn't necessary to make such contorted stretches of the imagination. Simply discard the notion that you have a single personality. Notice the variety that is you. You will find a lot of experiential validation when you drop the outmoded theory of one person—one personality. There are some who go even a step beyond Morita therapy and recommend that we drop the one-person theory altogether.

Individual Morita Growth Training

What is a Morita therapist like? What is it like to go through a course of Morita training in personal management? What are the benefits? How much work is involved? How is Morita training different from and similar to Western psychotherapies? Does it make sense to undertake Moritist guidance and a Western therapy at the same time? I commonly encounter such inquiries.

Typically, the student/client meets with the Morita therapist once a week for an hour. The principles contained in this book provide the major content of the teaching that occurs during these weekly sessions. The usefulness of training with a Moritist guide is that the general principles are revealed as they operate in the daily life of the particular student, their application is spelled out in a way that fits the individual needs of the student. Some of the students go on to do Moritist guidance of others, after completing a certification course of study.

I like to think of the Morita educator as a sort of tour guide. I am not a guru with astounding insight and powers to confer enlightenment, but I have traveled a course similar to that of my students. I can point out the scenery, the detours, and the most comfortable accommodations along this route toward the development of life skills. To carry the tour analogy a bit further, if we were riding a bus, each passenger would view the scenery through a different window, gaining a somewhat different perspective. But, in general, the highlights of our journey would be quite similar. Some people make the trip on their own. But for many it is reassuring to have someone along who has traveled the route, and who knows the points of interest to expect along the way.

Sometimes I make a mistake during a session. I misinterpret what I hear or I fail to communicate clearly. Mistakes lead to what needs to be done next, just as any act leads to a new situation with new requirements for action. Sometimes an apology, a clarification, or a question may be called for. But some of my students want me to be perfect. I can't be—for them, for myself, for anyone. Yet, I do provide a model of someone who keeps his eye out for what needs doing and gets on about doing it. Our Morita tour is, on the whole, a most interesting (though sometimes exhausting) one. I don't want to miss anything that is passing by.

The Moritist guide incorporates the principles of the training into his or her daily life. Because of this application, the ideas make perfect sense to him or her. They don't make perfect sense to the beginning clients, however. The new clients haven't tried them out, so they have no confidence that they are meaningful or workable. If I were to greet new students/clients with the perfectly good advice to accept suffering as it is and proceed with constructive action, well, I might not see them for a second visit.

Nearly everybody undergoes Moritist training initially in the hope of finding relief from some sort of hurt or pain (and unless they feel something is wrong, they may not be willing to commit themselves to trying out this demanding lifeway). They sense that there is a certain amount of hard work involved in mastering the principles. Often their vague goal is to feel good all the time, that elusive anxiety-free life. It takes a certain amount of time and training to demonstrate to them that there is something else, something even better than a placid life without conflict. That something is taking command of what they are doing no matter how they are feeling. Of course, they can't be expected to recognize this superior strategy at first.

When new clients enter training, I usually begin by showing them how close relief from distress has been and always is. That lesson they want to learn. I teach them about attention. Relief is only a microsecond away when their attention shifts from themselves and their suffering. The typical client immediately seizes upon this possibility of distraction from misery. Salvation is at hand, the client thinks. Indeed, the beginning trainee tries out active living and discovers during the first week or so that he or she does feel better. Terrific!

Furthermore, the client keeps coming back because Morita personal growth training offered something that worked, and worked quickly. He or she thinks there must be more that will work, too—and he or she is correct. There is something much more valuable to learn.

Of course, distraction doesn't really solve problems. Most often it only postpones some sort of confrontation with reality. Moreover, feeling good all the time isn't possible. Those who tell you that they are filled with joy every moment are either lying or to be pitied. How boring this unwavering feeling must be! Sooner or later the student/client begins to hear the message that there is something beyond immediate, temporary relief. He or she is ready then to begin building life on consistent, reality-based behavior rather than on evershifting feelings. There is still plenty of work ahead for both therapist/guide and student/client, but the foundation is usually laid firmly within six months.

This is the natural termination of Morita training. In about six months students have a good understanding of the basic principles. Weekly homework assignments have tested their ability to apply them outside the office setting. They begin to anticipate what I am likely to say when they come with a particular problem for discussion during our weekly sessions together. Studies by Tomonori Suzuki and Ryu Suzuki indicate that Moritist training can be accomplished in about six months, but maximum benefits are achieved after about twenty-four months from beginning therapy—in other words, it takes another eighteen months after terminating therapy to perfect the application of the principles in daily living. Clients in the United States sometimes wish to continue training beyond six months with less frequent contacts or to take the more intensive certification course to become Moritist guides. In any case, the work of applying Moritist attitudes and behaviors to finer and finer details of living continues indefinitely. Personal growth need never end. The tour goes on and on, with or without a guide.

DAVID K. REYNOLDS

The most effective Moritist guide maintains a balance between closeness and distance with the trainee. Students/clients need to know enough about the guide to be able to perceive that the teacher is an empathic companion. They need to know that their guide understands the sometimes tortured, bracketed lives that they lead. They need to see that he or she is enough like them to be able to say with confidence that because the Moritist lifeway works for the guide it will work for them as well.

Despite the empathy, the Moritist educator must retain some distance from the student. Morita therapy is directive. The guide must lead his or her students through the same sort of underbrush he or she has cleared away from his or her own life, encouraging them to clear their own paths. So the students/clients must be able to recognize that the guide isn't muddled in the same way that they are. The guide's goals are clear; there is a sort of transparency to living the Moritist life. Moritist guides know what needs to be done because they aren't floundering in feelings. Students/clients will notice the difference. That balance of familiarity and distance is used purposefully by the guide to accomplish the sensitive training that leads to the finest constructive living.

One difference between Moritist guides in America and some of those in Japan lies in the willingness of Westerners to use other therapy forms as adjuncts within an overall plan for constructive living. Some Japanese Morita therapists have taken a position opposing other therapy methods, particularly psychoanalysis. Morita himself engaged in debates against the naive Freudianism of his time. American Moritist educators, however, take a broader view of the matter. We frequently find alternative therapies useful for achieving certain therapeutic goals within our overall Moritist plans. Let us explore some of the ways in which Western therapy modes may be used to support an all-encompassing Moritist mode.

Psychoanalysis can be used to assist the client in recognizing and accepting feelings. Occasionally, we encounter students who do not accept their feelings as they are, in part because they don't recognize what they are feeling in a given moment. In particular, the client who denies, represses, and suppresses feelings may find free association and related psychoanalytic techniques useful in becoming aware of feelings so that he can accept them and examine them for information about what needs to be done. The awareness of feelings is not sufficient in itself to bring about needed changes in behavior and self-concept. Nevertheless, it can be a useful element in the total therapeutic program.

The original objections to the use of psychodynamic techniques within Morita therapy came from several misconceptions. One was that insight alone was considered by some to be sufficient for the eradication of neuroses. Morita correctly saw that such thinking was in error in most cases. Another misconception, one held by some early Japanese therapists, came from a too narrow view of the Moritist principle "doing what needs to be done." In early-twentieth-century Japan what needed to be done was defined in the strict terms of work tasks. Early Moritist guides saw anything that pulled their students' eyes away from moment-to-moment labor as a potentially dangerous distraction from constructive living. To free associate, for example—that is, to lie on a couch and speak aloud whatever thoughts and feelings came into one's mind—appeared to them to be focusing too much attention on the client's own symptoms and not enough on the world outside, which was filled with cues about necessary work.

Modern Moritists believe that early conceptions of what the world brings us to be done were too narrow and simplistic. Values aren't nearly so uniform today as they were in the Japan of seventy years ago. We are much more willing to accept the client's assessment of "what needs to be done" and to entertain such assessments as leisure activities, self-exploration, and personal growth in addition to fundamental self-sacrificing labor. Thus, when student and teacher agree that what needs doing is to work on a better understanding of what the student is feeling, then psychoanalytic or Gestalt techniques may be employed with no concern that they are anti-therapeutic or anti-Moritist.

Behavior training from behavior therapies can also make easier the "doing what needs to be done." Self-reinforcement regimens, self-behavior shaping, realistic use of extinction principles (letting a behavior fade over time because it goes unrewarded), avoidance of learning interference, and the like can be helpful in modifying the

DAVID K. REYNOLDS

Morita client's activity. But, Morita therapy is not the same as behavior therapy, although it can readily incorporate such techniques to aid in the solution of particular problems. In Morita therapy we are concerned with helping the client enter into the natural flow, so he can act appropriately to meet the needs of the present situation. But, there is no great advantage to *struggling* in order to meet these situational needs. If a person who overeats can stop overeating with relative ease using behavioral techniques, then that's fine. Again, we use the methods that work pragmatically to get the job done. However, changed behavior without acceptance of feelings and without clear purpose reduces the client to an automaton, pushed about by the therapist's purpose and technique. Behavior change alone is unsatisfactory.

An instructive parallel between Eastern and Western psychotherapy forms exists in Morita therapy and Rogerian nondirective therapy, in the area of acceptance of the patient. In Rogerian therapy, one task of the therapist is to accept the patient unconditionally, exactly as the patient is in that moment. However, this acceptance leads the Rogerian therapist to be nondirective, refraining from interpretation or explanation. Such acceptance is necessary in Morita therapy, too. The therapist is a model for the patient—demonstrating the acceptance of all of reality. Note that Moritists do not conclude from this acceptance of the patient that they should avoid influencing the patient to change. Far from it. The therapist is engaged in conspicuously attempting to influence the patient to change in constructive ways, all the while accepting the patient as he or she is.

This difference shows again the distinction that Moritists make between acceptance and passivity or acquiescence. Acceptance is the first step in making worthwhile changes in reality. *Arugamama,* or "accepting reality as it is," includes accepting patients as they are with whatever skills and faults and self-doubts and strengths they bring to therapy.

Logotherapy and other existential therapies help the client recognize life purposes, which may help the student find direction and meaning in life. Such exercises as writing one's epitaph, eulogy, and obituary weren't conducted in Morita's day. They, too, help the client examine life purposes. One potential danger of dwelling on long-term purposes is that some clients use them as an escape from everyday reality. They flee into exploration of these abstract, grand goals. Such investigations of life goals must be subjugated to the more disciplined, detailed exploration of purpose in moment-by-moment living in the present.

All these therapies that may be employed as adjuncts to Morita therapy are examples of the Moritist maxim "If it is raining and you have an umbrella, use it." They are umbrellas, useful tools to relieve some of the practical difficulties in achieving the goals of therapy. But none of them is sufficient in itself. Morita's theory as adapted in the United States fits these treatment elements into a unified whole. It provides a wholistic phenomenological perspective on suffering and personal development as well as an understanding of the effectiveness of all these therapies in terms of a single theory of flowing awareness and attention.

Morita therapy is built upon the concept of a lifeway. The attitude characteristic of this Moritist lifeway involves a feeling of participation with the world—with this sidewalk, with those abandoned tires, with that geranium. It is me as part of this scene; me as a piece of this jigsaw-puzzle world; me as observed observer, boundaried boundary, acting stage prop. This attitude contrasts with the notion that the world out there is performing for me. The traffic signals don't change for my frustration or joy; my favorite football team doesn't win for my elation. This latter perspective dichotomizes the world into that out there and me in here (with my all important desires and hopes). The concept of self is rather like the blinking cursor on the monitor of a computer. The cursor marks the place on the screen where something is happening. It is a pointer on the screen world to where something is taking place. But it remains a part of the total screen picture. We, too, are markers, locations, windows on reality.

The vision of the Moritist lifeway sees your joy as part of this moment/setting's joy and, therefore, it is part of my joy, too, as I participate in this moment/setting. We share this situated event. Your grief is mine also. We may feel exhausted at the end of a football game even though we participated in it only as spectators. With the fictional detective, we share the satisfaction of discovering the perpe-

DAVID K. REYNOLDS

trator of a crime in the latest mystery novel. We become one with our phenomenal environment; we fit ourselves into reality.

The further we move away from this participation in the world, the more we suffer unnecessarily. In our neurotic moments we do not lose ourselves in our surroundings. Instead, we lose ourselves in ourselves. We back off from the world into imagined dread, anticipated failure, worries about what might be or what might have been.

To love is to lose ourselves in another. It is to give up our lives for another, to abandon our former dreams as a sacrifice for another, to merge with that loved element of our environment. In other words, genuine love causes us to become part of our surroundings.

Sometimes I am asked, "Why endure negative feelings when it is possible to live in mild euphoria all of the time? It seems to me a rather petty goal in life merely to accept what one feels without aiming for constant happiness."

"Do you experience this state of constant euphoria? Is it truly possible, or is it something you have only read or heard about?" I ask the person. It is extremely rare to find anyone who claims to be in a state of constant bliss.

"Are you feeling this euphoria now?"

"Yes."

"Euphoria seems a rather strange emotion to be feeling in this situation, right now. More appropriate, it seems to me, would be keyed-up alertness, an intensity to help respond adequately to our discussion. Did you feel euphoric when a family member was seriously ill or when a friend died? I doubt it. Feelings need to fit particular situations, particular moments. A constant feeling has no meaning in terms of the changing events of everyday life."

Our Constitution grants us the right to the pursuit of happiness, but it seems unwise to pursue the elusive state. Better to pursue appropriateness or flexibility to adapt ourselves to reality and to adapt reality to fit our purposes as we participate in it.

Purposeful Living

A few years ago I met a man, Mr. Lewin, with a great dream and great energy. The dream itself was quite properly grand and worthy. What bothered me was that there was too much Lewin in Lewin's dream. It seemed that his fine purpose was confused with another, less significant one. It is important to be clear about our purposes. I must be careful about my purpose in writing this book, too. I want you to finish reading it with a fair sense of what Morita therapy is about. So I mix the theoretical with the personal and practical contents in order to avoid a presentation about the ideal as opposed to the real.

Throughout human history people have wondered about purposeful living, and there has been no lack of teachers to advise them about it: Plato, Confucius, Billy Graham, Dogen Zenji, Mao Tse-tung, Voltaire, and Norman Vincent Peale, to name just a few. However, there have been scores of lesser-known advisers in every age. In our era one large category of life guides are called psychotherapists. For all the use of medical jargon about mental illness, symptoms, diagnoses, and cures, therapists teach their "patients" a lifeway either explicitly or implicitly, either by direction or by model. There is an insightful book written by Perry London many years ago titled *The Modes and Morals of Psychotherapy*. In it London points out that every psychotherapeutic system contains a set of values, a definition of what it is to be fully human, and notions about suffering and the resolution of suffering. Psychotherapists, too, have purposes.

The purposes of Morita therapy are quite clear. They are, again, to teach students to accept feelings as they are, to know their purposes, and to do what needs to be done. All the other techniques of Morita's method are aimed at achieving these purposes or goals. For example, I may ask clients to report on the contents of their closets, or to describe the persons that they passed as they walked or drove to the therapy session, or to indicate where the fire exits are in buildings they have recently entered. These exercises help them to develop skills of observation. Observation helps us to be aware of what reality is bringing us to do in each moment. How can we be aware of what needs doing when we aren't paying attention to our circumstances? More advanced students not only notice their surroundings but begin to notice themselves as part of the surroundings and, ultimately, just to "notice." But that result goes beyond the modest goals of acceptance, purpose, and action.

Another technique of Morita therapy utilizes physical activity to accomplish tasks when we feel overwhelmed by feelings. You may have noticed that when you are upset it is more difficult to balance a checkbook and study a text than it is to wash your car or rearrange furniture or do the vacuuming. While we wait for our feelings to settle down, we need not turn off our lives; we can continue with constructive activity, getting done what needs doing. Somehow it's easier to keep our minds on tasks that require physical effort. A reminder: the purpose of doing a task is to get the task done (to get the dishes clean, to clear the weeds from the garden, to dust the bookcase), and *not* to distract ourselves from the feelings (although that may be a beneficial side effect).

Performing physical action as an aid to concentration is as useful for mental work like bookkeeping and studying as it is for vacuuming and gardening. When we underline, write out our thoughts on paper, outline the material we have read, or organize our desktop, we are likely to find it easier to attend to the mental task at hand. The more body movement aimed at achieving our goal (even the movement of hand holding pen, moving across paper), the better. The opposite approach, trying to keep every important point in mind, while merely exerting the will to keep the mind on a task, turns out to be less effective. For my office I have built a wooden podium that looks rather like a music stand. When I am tired from sitting in front of the computer, reading in the easy chair, or writing at the desk, I can stand and read at the podium, resting a book on it. Along the same lines, I sometimes conduct part of a therapy hour standing or walking alongside a student, especially when one or both of us is sleepy. Whatever our feelings (sleepiness, fatigue, rage, despair, fear), they need not distract us from purposeful behavior. And the behavior itself seems to pull us along toward our goals.

Morita therapists emphasize that it is important to find suitable constructive purposes and hold to them, thus guiding behavior in a positive direction. The other side of that coin is that all behavior, positive or negative, is purposeful. Whatever you do there is an aim to it, a goal toward which the behavior is directed. The goal may be destructive or constructive or mixed. For example, the shy person may avoid social gatherings *in order to* prevent the feelings of inadequacy and loneliness that he feels in such situations. In a sense Morita guidance asks the client to select constructive purposes and positive ways of achieving them instead of the already purposeful, but destructive behavior. Finding the purpose behind destructive behavior can be a useful undertaking because sometimes the original purpose can also be fulfilled in a positive way.

It is not a new idea that difficulties in life generate the construction of purpose. Happiness, peace, and a life of ease would destroy us. Without anxiety and trouble, we could not survive. Without conflict and struggle, life would not choose to continue. It is not that suffering is good; it is *necessary* for our existence. To say this is not to say that all pain must be passively accepted. We are responsible for doing battle with the ills that plague us and others. Yet, if we were ever to succeed in eliminating all discontent, our human species would be doomed. We struggle, and in that struggle lies life's meaning. We are born fighters; we will find something to oppose. If we cannot find a worthy foe, we create one, even if that foe is ourselves.

When our last enemy is vanquished, we shall die—as individuals, as a species.

So don't seek anxiety-free living; don't strive for constant bliss. Choose rather to continue your struggle. Resolve to react forcefully to the challenges of reality. Hold to your goals. Fight your fight. And live with purpose.

The Mythical Golden Hour

Sometimes I feel overwhelmed by the suffering of those around me, mostly that of my students/clients, but others as well. Showing them a way of relieving some of their unnecessary suffering is one of my survival techniques.

Sometimes, though, I don't feel like doing therapy. I would prefer to be off hiking in the Sierras or browsing through used-book stores or playing a set of tennis. Therapists may resist therapy, too. And, I find, some students are more likeable than others. My mood changes from day to day and hour to hour. Yet my profession requires that I be there for the student of therapy whether I am in the mood or not, whether the student is affable or not, whether therapy is progressing smoothly or not, and so on.

This path I have chosen; others depend on me. It is the same with all those in helping professions, I suspect. We are called upon to put out effort on a task even when we don't feel like it. *Why is it that our clients aren't taught this reality?* We experience the practicality of getting on about business day by day in spite of ups and downs of feelings. That lesson is central to our everyday lives. Patients need to hear it, to learn it. They need to know that we teach it not because of some distant psychodynamic theory but because we live it all the time.

I don't mind patients who feel resistance to Morita therapy. I do ·nind patients who demonstrate their resistance by failing to come to the therapy setting at the proper time. But those students who are dependably on time and show up for every training session are rare exceptions, less in need of the therapy for which they appear than many of their peers. Part of being neurotic is being irresponsible. Obsessive and compulsive patients are irresponsible, too. Irresponsible means self-centered. It means failing to notice or respond to what reality has brought that needs to be done. That reality includes other people. Neurotic people regularly inconvenience others by their actions.

Far from being too perfectionistic and self-conscious, the typical neurotics in my practice—both in the United States and in Japan—aren't perfectionistic and self-conscious enough! They dabble with guilt and feelings of inferiority without committing themselves to a course that would test and validate their superficial self-evaluations. They construct negative self-images more out of imagination than out of the realities of their behavior. When neurotics tell me that they should be less of something (less timid, tense, frightened, idealistic, perfectionistic, aware of aches and pains), it is fairly certain that they don't have enough of that very characteristic. They need more of it. They need enough to affect their behavior positively.

The neurotic goes part of the way and stops because of some initial discomfort rather than straightforwardly surmounting the obstacle. Because of the neurotic's skill at avoiding and imagining the results without testing them in reality, a set of unrealistic assumptions about the self, about pain, and about the consequences of behavior accumulates. All of us have visualized a confrontation blown up all out of proportion by our imaginations. When the confrontation (for example, having to return a purchased item, asking for or offering a resignation, negotiating a separation) finally occurred, it turned out to be unlike that which we had imagined. Having survived a few college examinations, breakups, refusals, job interviews, and flat tires, we become more confident that we can handle the next one. But the neurotic person, avoiding reality with its painful rejections, continues to build a picture of the world based less on overcoming difficulties than on imagining what it might be like to encounter them. Confidence cannot emerge from imagination-based escapes from real problems.

There is a myth in our culture that something magical occurs during an hour of psychotherapy. I call it the myth of the golden hour. Many people seem to believe that what happens during the golden hour of therapy is sufficiently powerful to color the rest of the week. They seem to believe that the other 167 hours of the week have less effect than that one hour. Even some therapists agree. To succumb to this myth is to relegate 167/168ths of life to meaninglessness. Life must be lived moment by moment. Each moment brings possibilities for purposeful activity. Each moment carries a message, a lesson for us. There are no golden hours, only ready people. When our attention is alert to notice what reality has brought us in this moment and to fit ourselves to it by doing what needs to be done, we are living fully during each of those waking hours.

In the practice of Morita therapy we extend the influence of the lessons about living beyond the therapy hour by use of homework assignments. The client may be asked to keep a journal of daily feelings and behaviors, to reflect on moment-by-moment purposes, to recall past debts and repay them, to write letters of concern or gratitude, to do exercises that sharpen attention, to conduct life according to a fixed temporary schedule, to prepare meals, explore unfamiliar supermarkets and parks, and so forth. The client may need to be reminded that salvation lies not in some golden hour of therapy but in the practice of daily life.

The hour of Moritist training each week becomes a model for the hours of the remainder of the week. The therapist listens, questions, advises, and instructs with full attention. I learned an important lesson about the impact of attentive listening from a Zen priest/physician named Usa in Kyoto, Japan. I went to his temple (now converted into a hospital) to conduct an interview concerning his practice of Morita therapy. After introductions were completed, I began with a few standard questions about his current practice. He listened carefully to my first question, then paused and seemed to be digesting what I had asked. Then he seemed to reply directly to the intent underlying my question. Soon, however, he answered succeeding questions with another question, and I shot back the first reply that came to mind. Each time, he paused and reflected on what he had heard and asked another question, which seemed to get at the heart of my research. Another superficial reply from me and another probing question from Dr. Usa and I had the feeling that he was "treasuring" my replies. I, too, began to pause before speaking. I began to select more carefully the words to offer him. After all, he was conscientiously and wholeheartedly mulling over each word; how could I present him with superficial responses for his efforts?

It was a strange feeling to be totally listened to; the physician/priest wasn't thinking of what would be served for dinner that evening or how many patients remained to be seen that day. He wasn't formulating his next question or constructing a reply as I spoke. He lost himself in what he heard. The intensity of his listening changed what I did. I began to take care in putting together my queries. I considered several directions for a response and selected the most suitable one before opening my mouth. His genuine listening had a powerful effect on me during that interview.

How difficult it is to duplicate the style of listening that this priest/physician/Morita guide showed me. I work hard at listening, only listening, fully listening to what my students say to me. Too often my mind has begun to analyze and prepare some comment before the student stops speaking. Sometimes I notice this intrusion and keep silent, turning attention back to the student's message. It is far less important to appear insightful and clever than to be fully involved in the hearing. The pauses are still too short. But I have felt the effect of being heard and want to share that experience with my students.

Through this listening, the assignments and the readings, the advice and the probing, I hope for a sort of transcendence for my students. The transcendence of which I write is no mystical experience. Instead, I wish for them something more modest from their Moritist training. I want them to transcend their emotions—to appreciate and acknowledge their feelings, but to be no longer governed by them, no longer fettered by them. To achieve this transcendence is to fulfill an important human potential. To strive for something beyond the transcendence of feeling without first mastering this human art is to skip an important step in one's development. It is like hoping for the harvest without watering or weeding the field.

Making Mistakes Pay Off

No one enjoys making mistakes. Mistakes are embarrassing, trouble-some, and frustrating—but they are great teachers. They teach us what worked and what didn't. They teach us the difference between theory and ideal on the one hand and reality on the other. They tell us that our attention was misdirected. They warn us of future embar-rassment and trouble and frustration, if we don't adjust to the reality that confronts us.

Some people are so sensitive to failure that they try to avoid mistakes at all costs. They try to act only in the safe areas of life, the areas that appear risk-free. They stand on the sidelines of living in order to reduce the possibility of failure. They don't realize that withdrawing from the exploration of life is a *big mistake*. Then, again, sometimes they do realize this truth. In those moments of recognition they envy others who seem to take setbacks in stride and wish that they, too, could move beyond the stifling bounds of as-sured safety.

There is an old Buddhist saying that the arrow that hits the bull's-eye is the result of the one hundred previous misses. We must keep on failing and correcting our aim until we are on target. Note that the person who quits after the ninety-ninth miss doesn't reap the benefits of all those previous mistakes. Accepting feelings of incompetence, we must nevertheless continue with what needs to be done.

In Morita therapy we emphasize that people learn about reality by acting on it. The dramas that we create in our imaginations about asking for a date or applying for the promotion or seeking the new job or moving to a new home do not inform us about reality as accurately as action does.

In Hawaiian Pidgin there is a much-used combined verb *try-see*. Try-see means just what it appears to mean—try a course of action and see what the results will be. Hawaiians don't talk about fantasy-see or daydream-see or sit-see because they are a practical people. Their language reflects a pragmatic, realistic view of the world.

Most published authors can give concrete illustrations of how numerous failures eventually became success. I have received my share of rejections from publishers—ranging from mimeographed forms to kind letters with thoughtful suggestions for revision. All of them taught me about what those editors and publishers didn't like or didn't publish. That information is useful, even though it hurts each time some perfectly marvelous piece isn't acknowledged as such by people who ought to know about what is publishable and what is not.

Similarly, some patients respond quickly to therapy and others drift away, apparently unchanged. I admit to some feelings of failure in these latter cases even though I know that, on the whole, I did my best and that they are ultimately responsible for the life course they choose. The work of E. Phillip Lakin offers hope that those who drop out of therapy need not be gratuitously considered therapy failures at all.

During the therapy hour, patients generously point out mistakes I make. Some have called me on not listening fully, for not truly hearing them. They have let me know when my eagerness to have them do what needs doing made me appear cold and unsympathetic to their suffering. Some of my errors in emphasis and illustration have been thoughtfully and perceptively pointed out by my students/patients. Yes, I am sometimes foolish and insensitive, sometimes distracted and lazy, but I will not give up this therapeutic enterprise for all my mistakes. The mistakes are not insignificant. But this work needs to be done, imperfect as it is.

Last night for dinner I ate a lettuce–Jell-O–grape salad, cut corn with pickled ginger in it, a spoonful of jelly in my bowl of chili, and raisins in a variety of dishes. There have been quite a few unsuccessful culinary experiments on my way to finding unusual and tasty food combinations. The variety is worth it to me. Risk and struggle are essential to life. I prefer to struggle with the ingredients of meals, rather than struggle with myself over some boring, restricted, oft-tested menu.

Elsewhere, I have characterized the Japanese as a society in which nearly everyone chooses the safest course because of the extreme fear of failure, particularly public failure. Years ago when I was teaching English conversation to Japanese students, it was difficult to get them to try out their English in front of the class. They were unwilling to practice in front of others for fear of displaying their faulty English. It was as if they wanted to speak English perfectly before trying it out. But if they spoke it perfectly, why attend an English conversation class? Many Japanese prefer to take the safe course throughout their schooling, into a recognized college, then into lifelong employment in a large, stable company. They marry conservatively with a traditional ceremony and have the acceptable pair of children, whom they raise in the standard way so that they, too, will grow up to be failure-proofed citizens.

This stereotyped description doesn't do justice to the variety of individuals in Japan, but I don't think the overall picture is grossly inaccurate. To Americans, whose culture has only recently emerged from the pioneer era, such a safety-oriented society appears rather uninteresting and repressive. In our westward expansion conservative, riskless values were subjugated to the need for gambles and exploration in order to open up the new land for a growing population. Failure, therefore, was a natural part of life for our forefathers. It still is today, though we feel we have more to lose now and so perhaps are more fearful of failure. We pay for our errors in all sorts of ways. Yet we need them. They teach us about our world and ourselves. Then, failure or success, the next moment brings us something that needs to be done. Swallowing error or accomplishment of the recent past, we turn to that next moment, always a fresh one, always carrying with it the possibility of new achievement.

DAVID K. REYNOLDS

Putting Life Off Until Tomorrow

One of our Moritist maxims is "Don't put your life on hold." While waiting for the results of a job interview or an examination, or even while stopped at a stoplight or waiting for the water in the teapot to boil, some people seem to turn off their minds, to drift along without noticing what reality is sending them during those "in-between" moments. Every moment is worthy of full attention and dedicated action; every moment holds the potential for use in building a character that is "realistic" in the finest sense of that word.

Putting off unpleasant or difficult tasks is a similar sort of habit with dysfunctional consequences. Not long ago a leaky radiator shot steam into a room in my home while I was out of town. I returned to find the paint peeling and flaking off the walls, and a support for a drapery rod had pulled loose from its anchor in the plaster. This situation is typical of the sort of task that won't go away; the room won't repair itself however much I might wish it to do so. Procrastination simply adds to my discomfort because I am repeatedly reminded of the difficult work awaiting me; the unsightly wall reappears each morning, and the struggle to get myself to do the task takes up increasing amounts of energy. In this case, there were a couple of days in which I had other commitments, so I was unable to get to the repair work immediately. On and off during those intervening days I felt rather out of sorts, recalling the scraping, repainting, and repairs that lay ahead.

The project took almost an entire day, but the result was rewarding, and the mental burden of the unaccomplished task, which had been carried for two days, disappeared. Reality doesn't bring us things to do according to some ideal schedule that we have planned in our minds. Sometimes it seems to be at the most inconvenient time that we are presented with a task that requires immediate attention. Cars break down, roofs leak, friends cry, weeds grow, dust accumulates, correspondence piles up, bills arrive, guests appear, and so forth. Jumping into reality, acting as the moment requires, eliminates some of the unnecessary suffering that accompanies procrastination and wishing that life were otherwise. Involvement in the doing not only moves us toward achievement of the immediate project, but it also distracts our attention from the foolish and unnecessary habit of focusing on our miserably bad luck.

We alone create neurotic struggles in life. Reality merely presents issues and problems for resolution. The neurotic struggles we experience are internal evaluations that we add to the circumstance presented to us. No architect ordains I will face 117 pleasant life operations and 114 unpleasant ones today. They simply come as they come and I define them so. Although we require challenges to live at our peak, to define these experiences as struggles and regret their persistence is unnecessary; it is our response to them that is vital.

To wait when action is necessary is a failure to respond to the needs of the situation. But, to act when waiting is the better solution is no better. Like many Westerners, I tend to lean toward action when inaction is more appropriate. I want a response from the world in my time frame, at my convenience. To be sure, I am willing to work hard to get the results I hope for. But working hard at waiting is difficult.

Notice I am careful to write about waiting and inaction rather than patience. It is true that I'm too often impatient. But patience is a feeling or an attitude or a state of mind. Patience is something that we have or don't have in any given moment. I can't create patience by my will any more than I can create love or courage. And you can't either. Patience may be developed indirectly through the act of waiting again and again. Patience is acquired over time, through attention to what we do. As we prune and nurture certain deeds, we indirectly influence what we think and feel. Thus, we change who we are. As a feeling, patience is no different. By waiting, we make ourselves into more patient people.

The kind of patience that we aim for in constructive living may be called "productive" patience. It is based upon productive waiting, which means being active in another area while waiting for some desired result. It means keeping our eyes off the pot that hasn't yet boiled. It means allowing our friends and mates time to work through their own thoughts and feelings and not forcing them to deal with issues according to our own timetables, our own convenience. It means allowing the glue time to set completely before testing it.

Productive waiting means asserting ourselves when necessary, but then cooly evaluating the outcome of our efforts and deciding what needs to be done next. Just as important, productive waiting means going about other business and play, while the situation is ripening. It means turning away fully, involving oneself wholeheartedly in some other pursuit, until the proper time comes to resume the attack on the problem. It means overcoming our obsessions with our time constraints, our concerns, and our convenience.

By "our convenience" here I am contrasting more than simply my convenience with that of someone else. The world about us has a timetable of its own. Events ripen at their own pace. Traffic moves along the freeway independent of my appointments and desires. I can choose to turn onto side streets if freeway traffic gets bottled up, but if I choose to stay on the freeway, I cannot ignore the speed of the cars around me moment by moment.

Perhaps some of you are expecting to read here some tips about how to comfortably and skillfully go about practicing this productive waiting. If so, I must disappoint you. I know of no easy way to keep my mind off those chocolate chip cookies baking in the oven. I have found, though, that putting my body in another room in front of some absorbing task makes the waiting somewhat more bearable. I have found also that the more I see productive waiting in actual living situations, the more I notice the payoffs, and the more I am willing to give this kind of waiting a try. Still, there is nothing I know of that makes waiting comfortable or easy in all situations.

I'll express it again: Moritist suggestions for living don't make life easy, but they make it sensible, and they put a handle on what is controllable in life. I mistrust anyone who offers constant happiness, endless success, instant confidence, or effortless self-growth. Somehow, those offers *never* get delivered.

Aesthetic Living

In the Japanese tea ceremony the simple serving of tea is brought to the culmination of aesthetic artistry. Each movement, from lifting the lid of the pot of boiling water to whisking the bitter-green powder into a frothy beverage, is studied and choreographed into an efficient and harmonious sequence. The tea guests, too, behave with precision and attention to detail. For example, when examining the beauty of the bowls for the tea, each guest holds the bowl only an inch or so over the tatami mats covering the floor and leans over to inspect the detail. The reason for bending over rather than bringing the bowl up to the eyes for easier examination is that these works of ceramic art are extremely valuable. If one should slip from the hand, it would fall only an inch onto a soft surface. Years of thinking have gone into the order of the movements. Every gesture is purposeful.

Putting away the dinner dishes can be a similar act of artistry. Or the movements in dressing and undressing, writing a letter or reading a newspaper, all these everyday activities can be carried out with the same purposeful care as that involved in the tea ceremony. To become a master of the tea ceremony takes years of diligent practice. To become a master of everyday living takes much longer, but it is much the same process. What are the benefits of this concern with the aesthetics of the mundane?

It is said that a certain frame of mind is developed during the tea ceremony. It is not that the participant necessarily brings this frame of mind to the ceremony. More often it is the participation in the ceremony that creates receptivity to the aesthetic of the moment. Once again, the principle of action preceding attitude or emotion applies. That is why in feudal times Japanese aristocracy scheduled tea ceremonies when they were upset or in need of careful thought before making a major decision. Executing the deliberately paced, well-practiced movements returned the mind to a serene state. Haven't you done the same with a long, quiet drive when you were upset or before making some important decision? Haven't you ever felt the peace that comes from preparing a traditional meal or knitting a familiar pattern or grooming a pet? The familiarity, the rhythmic, patterned behavior, the pulling of one's attention into an intimate task, all work to produce a clear and calm mind. Anxious, rattled feelings fade before the systematic, measured movements of the body.

Trust

You may wonder where the element of trust or faith enters into the Moritist lifeway. Is this method so rational, so scientific that there's no need for elements of belief? Actually, there are points for which trust is necessary, but these points don't call for blind trust. They involve trust based on experience. That is, one must trust the method initially in order to give it a serious try, and then the results will reinforce one's confidence in the undertaking. We can break down this trust further into the following statements:

1) We trust the world to keep producing some reality to which we can attend. We believe that there is a reality out there calling for our response. It isn't created by our imagination; it doesn't respond directly to what we wish or feel. It responds to what we do. Reality isn't fair or just in any simple, apparent sense. But it does seem to be orderly and more or less understandable and predictable as we study it.

2) We trust the inner prompting that tells us what needs to be done in the moment. The clarity of this inner voice improves as we listen and respond to it. We learn to distinguish it from the fleeting impulses and thrashing about of undisciplined mental play. Many people work hard to avoid noticing what needs to be done because when they notice the requirements of reality they are confronted with the necessity of doing something about

them. What they don't notice, they think they aren't responsible for. The strength and guidance of our inner prompting gives direction to our lives. Life takes on special meaning as we go about living it attentively.

3) We trust our ability to control our own behavior regardless of our feelings. This trust, too, comes after we've done what needed doing in spite of and in concert with our feelings. When the feelings merely provide interesting information instead of determining our behavior, we are free to act as reality demands. "Our ability" can be discovered only after we've accomplished something, not before. *After I* control my behavior, I can confidently say that I possess the ability to control it. Why bother with such analysis of our abilities at all? Analysis or not, we assume control of our behavior regardless of our feelings.

4) We trust the appropriateness of merging ourselves with our circumstances and situation. The opposite approach brings disharmony and unnecessary struggle and suffering. When we adapt ourselves to the needs of this moment, we become part of the moment itself. There is no resistance through wishing life were otherwise, no longing for the ideal or for what ought to be. Rather there is constructive action to use this situation to bring us closer to our ideal reality. This constructive action affects both the situation in which we find ourselves and the "me" who acts on the situation. We keep coming closer together, reality and I.

5) We trust that others' experiences are enough like our own to be helpful. The Moritist lifeway keeps showing how we are like others rather than how we are different from them. As we listen with full attention to what others tell us, we begin to notice the similarities between their reality and our own. Their anxiety looks more and more like ours, their struggles resemble ours. With training, we almost seem to become them for periods of time. In other words, they become part of the situation with which we merge. This merging is rather like what is called empathy, though it is broader, encompassing objects and other phenomena as well as people.

6) Finally, we trust our judgment of what is effective in contributing to a satisfying, meaningful life. What works in a prag-

DAVID K. REYNOLDS

matic way we are sensible enough to value. What doesn't work we are sensible enough to revise or discard. Our trust won't lead us to foolish belief in a lifeway that isn't practical. We keep testing Morita's ideas against reality. We trust our evaluations of what is realistic in the purest sense of that word.

Heads You Lose, Tails You Lose

I just had a call from a client who was feeling terrible because the cashier at the Motor Vehicle Department treated him so well. He felt that he didn't deserve such kind treatment.

"I wonder how you would have felt if she had treated you badly," I mused.

"Probably terrible," he confessed.

I suspect he was right. He's set up a no-win situation for himself.

Dr. Takehisa Kora, a prominent Moritist in Tokyo, tells the story of a patient who came to him complaining that he feared going insane. Kora examined the man and explained that he wasn't going insane, rather he was suffering from a sort of phobia about going insane. He also told the patient that people who actually do go insane generally do so without awareness, and those who worry about insanity never go crazy; worrying in that characteristic way is almost a guarantee that it won't happen. The man felt reassured.

However, a couple of weeks later the patient returned with a new complaint.

"I'm not so anxious now about going crazy. So I wonder if I'm not in danger now of really going crazy."

Heads he loses, tails he loses.

Newness and change provoke no-win responses from some people. They are uncomfortable in their current situations, but they dread the unknown elements of change, too. To stand still is to be in pain; to move is to create pain.

One professor I know had an irrational fear that by reading high-level theoretical material he would be caught up in a world of intriguing ideas and so lose touch with reality. He recognized that the fear was probably groundless, but it was the very "groundlessness" that left him trembling with fascination and terror. If he didn't keep up to date, he was doomed professionally. If he read, he risked drifting off into ethereal realms, permanently.

What these people have in common is that they let their thinking freeze their action. They are immobilized by trying to take into consideration what might happen. They want to figure out all the angles beforehand. They want to be assured that every future step is safe, pain free. But life offers no such guarantees. So what can they do?

They must act anyway, without confidence, without assurance, without a clear view of all possible outcomes. We don't need to know everything about everything before putting our bodies in motion. Careful consideration is worth our time and attention, but straddling the fence waiting for everything to become absolutely clear offers only saddle sores. If you are in pain, take the constructive step into the unknown and discover what reality has in store for you in the next moment.

Talk

Talk provides us with great mobility in our interactions. It moves us from the here and now to the past and the future; it moves us from the concrete to the general and abstract. It reveals who we are and conceals who we are. Within the psychotherapy session, talk has the potential of allowing the patient to escape from this here-and-now reality.

Ms. Fox sprinkles words like *ventilate, altercations, emotional outbursts, relating,* and phrases like *communicative relationships, fraught with possibilities, raising the intention level,* and *analyzing the ego structure* throughout her speech during our sessions. I ask her what her purpose is in doing so.

Mr. Smith makes an attempt to talk only about last month's events during the therapy hour. He offers wide-view descriptions, distanced analytic interpretations. I ask him what he ate for breakfast this morning. He tells me that his symptoms affect his job performance. I ask him how, specifically, and when was the last time they had such an effect and what he did then.

Mr. Lamb breaks into tears as we look at the details of his running away from Ellen and Corinne and Meredith and Eunice. I hand him the box of tissues. "I have choices," he says, sniffling. "What choices? Name your choices." He replies with a long-term goal. I ask what steps he must take today to move toward that goal. He shifts into musing about why he has trouble relating to women. I wonder aloud what he means by "relating," say, in the case of Eunice.

Mrs. Hopper can offer many reasons why she didn't write in her journal during the week. Some of the analysis is fascinating. The reality is that she didn't write. What did she do—yesterday, for example? She was so busy, she states. But when we consider in detail what events occurred yesterday, we find that the generalization that she didn't have time to write in her journal is completely refuted. In fact, she had a great deal of time on her hands. Without resisting for a moment, Mrs. Hopper shifts to plans for the future: "I think I'm going to . . ." When? How? She decides that she needs more motivation, more commitment to do the journal. I tell her that she needs neither, she simply needs to write in the journal. Would she like to write an entry in the journal right now? She objects that this is the therapy hour. Writing in the journal isn't what needs to be done now? Fine. "What do you see as needing to be done in this moment?" I ask.

Mr. Crane wants answers, but sees that there are none. He remarks that he hasn't ever gotten his life together for any period of time. Then he examines what he has said and retracts the generalization. We spend some therapy time cleaning his room. He asks me to give an example of a Moritist principle. I do. He wants instant insights, and I ask him what he needs to do next. He begins to ask the situation what needs to be done next. It is a fruitful session.

Talk, talk, talk. How often it is used to back away from reality. How difficult it is to use it to approach reality. How important it is to truly listen to the talk.

Gestalt Therapy Parallels

Some psychotherapists have noted similarities between the Gestalt therapy as developed by Frederick S. "Fritz" Perls and Morita therapy. There are, in fact, a number of parallels between the two therapeutic systems. Indeed, in his autobiography Perls includes an account of a short stay in a Morita therapy hospital in Japan. And, in spite of occasional misinterpretations, Perls picked up enough from his experience with Zen and Morita therapy to incorporate some of the ideas into his Gestalt psychotherapy. One can easily see an occasional Zen story and phrase in his lectures and writings. I will quote a number of passages from his writing in order to point out commonalities with Moritist thought.

I have no doubt that Perls arrived at some of these ideas independently, after all, he (like Morita) was building his system in part inductively, on the basis of his experiences and the phenomenological reports of his patients. Historical primacy, however, must go to Morita, who was writing about his system from 1917 until the early 1930's. Perls's earliest writings were in the 1950's.

The following extracts with page numbers are from *Gestalt Therapy Verbatim* and those without are from the unnumbered pages of *In and Out of the Garbage Pail,* both by Fritz Perls. All emphases are in the originals.

Morita therapists speak of accepting reality as it is and including ourselves as part of that reality. Such acceptance doesn't involve apathetic resignation; on the contrary, it is the first step toward constructive change. Struggling with ourselves, chiding ourselves for not being the ideal persons we'd like to be, merely distracts us from responding effectively to what reality has brought us in this moment. Perls, too, recognized this essential step of self-acceptance.

The fact that we live only on such a small percentage of our potential is due to the fact that we're not willing . . . to accept myself, yourself, as the organism which you are by birth, constitution, and so on. You do not allow yourself . . . to be totally yourself. (p. 11)

Leave this to the human—to try to be something he is not—to have ideals that cannot be reached, to be cursed with perfectionism so as to be safe from criticism, and to open the road to unending mental torture.

Acceptance of reality as it is implies paying attention to it. Reality keeps urging that which needs to be done. Moritist guides suggest to their clients/students that they accept feelings as they are and get on with doing what needs to be done in the current situation. Perls wrote of this necessity, too:

If you understand the situation which you are in, and let the situation which you are in control your actions, then you learn how to cope with life. (p. 19)

Kondo Akihisa, who utilizes both psychoanalytic and Moritist methods in his Tokyo practice, emphasizes Morita's realization that neurotic patients frequently try to substitute intellect for experience. They seek to understand and control with their minds. And Perls writes:

We discover that the meaning of life is that it is to be lived, and it is not to be traded and conceptualized and squeezed into a pattern of systems. (p. 3)

Kondo points out that far from being ascetic, Morita's lifeway is rather epicurean. As he puts it, "It is tasting the best fruits of life." Here, too, is the admonition to live life fully, rather than allowing the mind to create paralysis.

Perls shared with Morita therapists distrust of any reliance on verbal instruction alone. This distrust is related to the point that life's richness is to be found in living it, not in solely thinking or talking about it. Like Perls, the Moritist guide goes beyond explanation to construct situations and assignments in which experiential learning takes place. Contact with reality carries potential for teaching lessons that need to be learned.

> You wouldn't learn from my words. Learning is discovery. There is no other means of effective learning. You can tell the child a thousand times, "The stove is hot." It doesn't help. The child has to discover it for himself. And I hope I can assist you in learning, in discovering something about yourself. (p. 26)

The concern with the reality of the present moment pervades Zen Buddhism and Morita therapy. We have nothing but the now. This moment and this reality are all that is presented to us for our action. Here and now presents our only hope for constructive change. And Perls writes:

> Whenever you leave the sure basis of the now and become preoccupied with the future, you experience anxiety. (p. 30)

> Whether you remember or anticipate, you do it *now*. The past is no more. The future is not yet. (p. 41)

In the following quote we would not use the words "getting in touch with," but our goals in Morita therapy wouldn't be far from those of Perls. By noticing and accepting what is occurring, the patient pulls himself out of his mental wheel spinning and into reality.

> By getting in touch with environment and self, the patient learns to differentiate between his fantasies and his assessment of reality.

Any viable psychotherapeutic system must provide a clear understanding of the relative responsibilities of therapist and client. While both Moritists and Gestalt therapists are concerned with the choices their clients make in life, they are clear that the clients must take full responsibility for their own actions. This attitude is not merely for the protection of the therapists or for the growth of the clients. It is based on the reality that I cannot control others in any direct and lasting way, so I cannot accept responsibility for their actions. I may teach, but whether my students learn is quite another matter.

I usually tell the group that I am not taking any responsibility for anyone except myself. I tell them that if they want to go crazy or commit suicide, that if this is their "thing," then I would prefer it if they would leave the group.

Responsibility means the ability to respond: the ability to be alive, to feel, to be sensitive. . . . In other words, responsibility is the ability to respond and be fully responsible for oneself and for *nobody else*. This is, I believe, the most basic characteristic of the mature person. (p. 100)

The title of this book, *Playing Ball on Running Water,* is taken from a Zen koan that deals with constant change. The Greeks, too, recognized that we can't step into the same river twice. Change is fundamental to our universe, from interstellar events to the decay of subatomic particles. The reality of our experience is in constant flux, too. Feelings come and go, impulses rise and disappear, thoughts flit through our minds. Our actions, Moritists hold, contain the possibility for influencing the course of this change. The actions may not control change, but they affect it. Perls had the glimmerings of our experience of playing ball on running water.

What happens is that the idea of deliberate change *never, never, never* functions. . . . Changes are taking place by themselves. If you go deeper into what you are, if you accept what is there, then a change automatically occurs by itself. This is the paradox of change. . . . As soon as you make a decision, as soon as you want to change, you open up the road to hell because you can't achieve it, so you feel bad, you torture yourself, and then you start to play the famous self-torture game which is so popular with most people in our time.

As long as you fight a symptom, it will become worse. If you take responsibility for what you are doing to yourself, how you produce your symptoms, how you produce your illness, how you produce your existence—the very moment you get in touch with yourself—growth begins, integration begins. (p. 178)

Morita therapy proposes that in order to escape unnecessary suffering we must learn what is controllable in life and what is not. Our feelings, our symptoms of doubts and fears and anxiety and obsessions, aren't directly controllable by our will. Neither are our spouses, lovers, rivals, employers, and neighbors. To be sure, we can do what we can to influence them all, but there is no guarantee that what we do will have the effect for which we hope. When we accept the reality of what is and what is not possible, we stop pressuring ourselves to achieve the unachievable. Perls, too, recognized the irrational push within us to control the uncontrollable.

If you feel you have to control everything, immediately you feel impotent. For instance, the very moment I want to crawl up the wall, here, I am bound to feel impotent. (pp. 211–12)

Perls's solution to the tendency to run from pain seems rather Western, bold, and even counterphobic. He recommends diving into the troublesome dilemma. I am not sure that such an aggressive approach is always necessary. Moritists share with the Gestaltists the opinion that avoiding and fleeing from symptoms only leads to increased difficulties. However, acceptance of myself along with my limitations is sufficient to permit facing unpleasant feelings. So, rather than telling sufferers to rush headlong into distress, Moritist guides suggest doing what can be done to alleviate the circumstantial pressures that cause discomfort. We believe that acceptance and realistic action are sufficient, without attacking the dragon, as Perls advises. Again, we agree that resistance is fruitless. The principles of aikido and judo are similar here. One accepts the force of the opponent without resistance. While yielding to it one goes about doing what needs to be done to throw the opponent to the ground.

Morita called his method reeducation. He saw that neurotic habits were learned misdirections of natural and positive tendencies found in all humans. Rather than needing a psychiatrist/physician, neurotic persons need an educator/guide. They need to learn a viable lifeway, a realistic perspective on living. Again, we find the echo in Perls.

> I consider the neurosis to be a symptom of incomplete maturation. This could possibly mean a shift from the medical to the educational point of view, and it would include a reorientation of the behavioral sciences.

Many of the Moritist maxims deal with the naturalness of feelings. For example, "Feelings are for feeling," "Suffering got us here," "Suffering grows from a seed of beauty," "Pain brings us to the present," and "Worry provokes planning" are reminders that, however unpleasant a feeling may be, it is useful and "proper" given the context in which it occurs. It can call our attention to something that needs to be done. Perls, too, remarked on the utilitarian nature of emotions.

> Nature is not so wasteful as to create emotions as a nuisance. Without emotions we are dead, bored, uninvolved machines.

Another quality of feelings that is emphasized in Morita therapy is their transitory nature. "Feelings are changeable, like the Japanese sky—sometimes cloudy, sometimes sunny," the Japanese therapists are wont to say. "So build your life on what is controllable, something that has more lasting results; build your life on what you do." In *The Quiet Therapies,* I devoted a section to the strange American ideal of being happy all of the time. But, happiness comes and fades like any other feeling. The rich variety of feelings "are for feeling." As Perls put it:

> You cannot *achieve* happiness. Happiness happens and is a transitory stage. Imagine how happy I felt when I got relief from bladder pressure. How long did that happiness last?

Shyness is one of the most common symptom complexes encountered in Japan. Morita therapy is quite effective with the anthropophobic patient (one who suffers from discomfort in social situations). The self-focus of the anthropophobic patient also shows clearly in Perls's analysis. However, the Moritist doesn't try to explain the symptoms as Perls does, using the psychoanalytic concept of projection.

In sum, we find a number of parallels between Gestalt therapy and Morita therapy and some key differences. To whatever degree Perls's ideas were borrowed or stimulated by Moritist thought they were reformed within an original, psychoanalytically based system in a manner understandable and appealing to Westerners. Just as H. B. Gibson, writing in *Behavior Research and Therapy* magazine, recommended the possibility of fruitful exchange between Morita therapists and behavior therapists, I believe that the exchange of ideas between Gestalt therapists and Morita therapists would be mutually beneficial.

Deciding to Decide to Decide

When one looks below the surface symptoms, the typical neurotic person found in Japan and most commonly treated by Morita therapy isn't particularly different from the sort of neurotic person we see in the United States. Abe Toru, a leading Morita therapist at the famous Kora Koseiin Hospital, described the characteristics of the Japanese *shinkeishitsu* neurotic person. I find it useful to read his description to my new patients in the United States. It helps them to realize that they are not alone in their misery, that their tendencies are shared even by members of another culture.

Abe notes that *shinkeishitsu* neurotics tend to be persistent. On the one hand, their persistence is a positive trait in that they can stick to a situation in an attempt to finish it or get through it. On the other hand, the persistence may appear as an obsession; they cannot let go of an idea or course of action, even when it is no longer useful. These neurotic people tend to be affected physiologically whenever there are changes or stresses in their lives. Headaches, insomnia, upset stomach, diarrhea, heart palpitations, loss of appetite, general weakness, and lethargy characterize their bodies' response to pressures from their environment.

They often have self-doubts. Is this course of action all right? Did I do it properly? What do others think of me? Such concerns are common with adolescents, but neurotically oriented people tend to spend more time thinking about such things, worrying about them.

They find themselves unsatisfied even when reassured that they are doing quite well. As they grow older, their perfectionistic and idealistic inclinations continue. They demand more than one hundred percent from themselves and from others, too. This makes relations with others difficult. Not only do they criticize themselves for failing to live up to their own standards, they demand perfection in others.

Abe further observes that these neurotic people are disposed to all-or-nothing thinking. They don't want to undertake something unless they are absolutely confident that they can accomplish it. Sometimes they stop a project in midstream because they discover that it is more difficult than they had believed at first. When they ask for advice, they want a clear choice: either A or B. They don't like the muddied gray areas of life.

Abe, like Perls, noted that neurotic people are self-protective. Much of what they do can be understood in terms of their wanting to avoid pain. These efforts lead them into further trouble and further dissatisfaction with their lives. As they move into middle age, the symptoms may shift from obsessions and phobias to anxiety neuroses. Anxiety neuroses generally revolve around the fear of death or loss of ordinary consciousness—heart palpitations cause the person to fear a heart attack, dizziness provokes ruminations about a stroke. These anxiety "attacks" seem to appear out of nowhere, with no obvious precipitating circumstance. Some of my clients have them frequently just before bedtime.

Something that I have noticed about *shinkeishitsu* people in both the United States and Japan is that they try to turn every action into a decision. They make every act a psychological dilemma. The reality is that nothing is getting done except deciding. They are really deciding to decide, not deciding to act. By this process they push themselves away from reality into their own minds.

Neurotic people of this sort are rarely stupid. They may have strange impulses and random thoughts about leaping down the stairs or stripping themselves in front of a crowd, but they're not the kind of people who actually do crazy and wild or hurtful and malicious things. For all their fantasies and worries, they tend to behave pretty conservatively. For the most part, I can trust my clients' judgment about what needs to be done. Until they demonstrate otherwise, I assume that they are competent. You need not trust your own judgment, but if you act on it and events work out all right, most of the time, then just continue to stumble along like the rest of us—without confidence some of the time, but doing what needs doing nevertheless.

Expanding Symptoms

In a recent issue of *Seikatsu no Hakken* ("The Discovery of Life"), one of the Moritist magazines in Japan, a member of the Moritist mental health organization described his food-related neurosis. His story illustrates the typical way in which neurotic symptoms expand to take over more and more of the sufferer's daily life.

It began for Mr. Morikawa in the ninth grade. On the way home from school one day he stopped with a friend to eat. While waiting to be served, he noticed four or five adults enter the restaurant and he felt somewhat intimidated and self-conscious because they seemed so at ease in this public place. The discomfort made him lose his appetite and, feigning illness, he complained of a stomachache and fled home without eating.

On arriving home he was disgusted with himself for not being able to eat, even though his stomach had been empty. Self-criticism and self-doubts filled his mind. After that event he began to feel uncomfortable whenever he had to eat with others. So he began avoiding dining in public. When he couldn't avoid it, he spent hours in anxious anticipation of the terrible experience awaiting him.

In high school he saw many motion pictures and confused the smoothness of action and speech presented in those fantasies with reality. In other words, he expected himself to be able to speak and move with the grace and confidence of the actors he saw on the screen. His ideals for himself were unrealistic. His inability to meet these fantastic standards caused greater timidity and feelings of inferiority.

During his senior year in high school, Mr. Morikawa's father became bedridden with illness. So the young man was forced to go to work right after graduation. As a company employee, he encountered many situations in which he was expected to eat with others. Some of them he couldn't avoid. He continued to eat lunch alone at his desk, but during company training programs he had to eat lunch in the presence of his fellows. At such times he worried for days ahead about his plight, lost his appetite, and missed all that was said during the morning's training session.

He continued to deride himself for his cowardice. When the noon meal was served during training, the mere smell of the food nauseated him, and he was unable to eat. In time Mr. Morikawa began to feel his stomach churning, even when he ate alone. Furthermore, whenever he felt self-conscious or anxious for any reason, the nausea appeared. Finally, when his parents simply looked at him, he felt upset and in need of medicine to keep his food down. He ate less and less, only enough to keep himself alive.

Mr. Morikawa looked ahead with despair to year after year of this suffering. He worried that he would eventually die from nutritional deficiencies. Thoughts of death began invading his mind, and feelings of inferiority increased. He began to stutter noticeably. Answering the telephone became an anxiety-provoking chore. He wanted to quit work, but couldn't, because of financial considerations.

Here we consider a young man who could trace many of his food-related problems to one event when he fled from eating in a public restaurant because of his discomfort in that social situation. Of course, that event was not the whole of the cause of his neurosis. Nevertheless, the extension of his symptoms from public eating to private eating, from the dread event itself to apprehension of the event, from food to fears of death are clearly displayed.

There is no insight, no psychotherapeutic technique that will make Mr. Morikawa's discomfort disappear in a flash. A positive life course and a positive self-image will come only after he has faced these discomforting life situations over and over and continued with constructive action in spite of his fears and worries. He can outgrow (and has) much of his neurosis. However, this doesn't necessarily mean he always feels relaxed when eating in public with his fellows. But there is no way to develop confidence in such situations other than by living through them with more positive goals and attitudes. As Mr. Morikawa learns to lose himself in noticing the decor of the café, listening to the revelations of his friends, savoring the taste of the food, and working toward helping others have a pleasant eating experience, his symptoms will shrink to more normal proportions.

Action Prepares

Constantin Stanislavski, director of the Moscow Art Theater, left the legacy of Method to the acting profession. His work in the theater occurred during approximately the same period Morita was putting his ideas into practice in Japanese psychotherapy. Two accomplished men with different professions in two countries offered surprisingly similar insights into human emotions. Stanislavski aimed at directing his acting students toward the emotions required by the parts that they played onstage. But, then, "All the world's a stage, And all the men and women merely players."

The quotes below are from Stanislavski's *An Actor Prepares.* They are interspersed with parallel concepts and comments based on Morita therapy. All emphases are in the original.

Neurosis, in Moritist terms, is nothing other than that sidetracking of attention and misdirection of energy and action. According to Stanislavski, the actor's larger purpose of the moment is to perform well. Acting is what the actor has decided needs to be done at the moment. It is a specific case within the larger domain of doing what needs doing.

Feelings are uncontrollable directly by the will, Morita held. Stanislavski, the master of generating feelings, agrees. Moritists note that feelings are changeable, "like the Japanese sky; sometimes cloudy, sometimes sunny." It is necessary, therefore, to find some indirect way of influencing emotion. Even the methods employed by these teachers to affect the effect are the same.

"... It would be wonderful if we could achieve a permanent method of repeating successful emotional experiences. But feelings cannot be fixed. They run through your fingers like water. That is why, whether you like it or not, it is necessary to find more substantial means of affecting and establishing your emotions." (p. 144)

The use of action to influence feelings is also found in Stanislavski's methods.

"... *On the stage there cannot be, under any circumstances, action which is directed immediately at the arousing of feeling for its own sake.* To ignore this rule results only in the most disgusting artificiality. *When you are choosing some bit of action leave feeling and spiritual content alone.* Never seek to be jealous, or to make love, or to suffer, for its own sake. *All such feelings are the result of something that has gone before. Of the thing that goes before you should think as hard as you can. As for the result, it will produce itself.* ..." (p. 38)

Experiential learning was valued by both Stanislavski and Morita. Both recognized the usefulness of intellectual understanding, but saw with equal clarity its limits as well. Action brings a particular sort of knowledge in which the response of our surroundings acts as teacher.

In Morita therapy, we teach the students to pay attention to their surroundings. This attentiveness pulls them from their excessive self-centeredness and enriches their lives. In addition, noticing the world around increases their sensitivity to what needs to be done in the moment. Stanislavski told his actors:

"If I ask you a perfectly simple question now, 'Is it cold out today?' before you answer, even with a 'yes,' or 'it's not cold,' or 'I didn't notice,' you should, in your imagination, go back onto the street and remember how you walked or rode. You should test your sensations by remembering how the people you met

DAVID K. REYNOLDS

were wrapped up, how they turned up their collars, how the snow crunched underfoot, and only then can you answer my question." (p. 67)

Training to fully focus one's attention results in not a normal life but a superior one. I am not particularly interested in bringing subnormal lives up to par, but rather in aiding the development of exceptional ones. The very qualities that contributed to the development of neurotic fixations of attention are the qualities that will push the guided client on to a superior life-style. Morita noted the potential for superiority in his patients. Stanislavski did likewise for his actors:

"An actor should be observant not only on the stage, but also in real life. He should concentrate with all his being on whatever attracts his attention. He should look at an object, not as any absent-minded passerby, but with penetration. Otherwise his whole creative method will prove lopsided and bear no relation to life. . . .

"Average people have no conception of how to observe the facial expression, the look of the eye, the tone of the voice, in order to comprehend the state of mind of the persons with whom they talk. They can neither actively grasp the complex truths of life nor listen in a way to understand what they hear. If they could do this, life, for them, would be better and easier, and their creative work immeasurably richer, finer, and deeper. But you cannot put into a person what he does not possess; he can only try to develop whatever power he may have. In the field of attention this development calls for a tremendous amount of work, time, desire to succeed, and systematic practice.

"How can we teach unobservant people to notice what nature and life are trying to show them? First of all they must be taught to look at, to listen to, and to hear what is beautiful. . . . Nothing in life is more beautiful than nature, and it should be the object of constant observation. . . . And do not shun the darker side of nature. Look for it in marshes, in the slime of the sea, amid plagues of insects, and remember that hidden behind these phenomena there is beauty, just as in loveliness there is unloveliness. . . ." (pp. 86–87)

It has been argued from a Moritist perspective that neurotic suffering is nothing other than a problem of attention. Attention difficulties seem to lie at the root of acting problems, too. As Stanislavski wrote:

> "Remember this: all of our acts, even the simplest, which are so familiar to us in everyday life, become strained when we appear behind the footlights before a public of a thousand people. That is why it is necessary to correct ourselves and learn again how to walk, move about, sit, or lie down. It is essential to re-educate ourselves to look and see, on the stage, to listen and to hear." (p. 73)

> ". . . Your attention will slip and become dissipated in space. *You must collect it again and redirect it as soon as possible to one single point or object. . . .*" (p. 80)

> "Strained attention shackles you every bit as much as muscular spasms. . . . " (p. 272)

Agreement can be found on a more philosophical point in the writings of these two men. Both anchored their understanding of truth not in some absolute ideal "out there," but in the phenomenological reality of the individual. That knowledge of truth, built up from life experience, provides the groundwork for the actor's construction of his part and the patient's construction of his cure. Stanislavski wrote, ". . . *in ordinary life, truth is what really exists, what a person really knows. . . .*" (p. 121) And he extends this phenomenological base to parallel considerations of the self, as well.

> "Where do you leave off and where does your part begin?"
> "That's impossible to say," answered Vanya, perplexed. (p. 289)

> "An actor's attention is constantly passing from one object to another. It is that constant change of foci that constitutes the unbroken line. . . ." (p. 244)

DAVID K. REYNOLDS

In other words, the self *is* that unbroken flow of attention. There is no other way to make sense of Stanislavski's admonitions to be both yourself and the part. The flow of attention is both. Although Morita didn't explicitly write about multiple selves, his system is developed from Zen Buddhist thought with its fundamental disaffection with the concept of a consistent self. Both he and Stanislavski disapprove of the notion that we have unchanging characters, but agree that we are eminently flexible in terms of feelings, behavior, and objects of attention.

It follows as a sort of corollary that solutions to many of life's problems come not from struggling with them, but from merging with them, adapting to them, accepting them for what they are. Such has been the advice given by Moritists since the earliest days. About this Stanislavski wrote:

He further explained what he meant by adjusting or conforming oneself to a problem. (p. 211)

"You must learn to adapt yourselves to circumstances, to time, and to each individual person. . . ." (p. 215)

Typically, the beginning student of acting or of psychotherapy is mistaken about what is possible and desirable as a result of the training. Stanslavski wrote:

"What more do you ask for. . . ."
Then I confessed my longing to be inspired.
"Don't come to me for that. My 'system' will never manufacture inspiration. It can only prepare a favourable ground for it.
"If I were you, I would give up chasing this phantom, inspiration. Leave it to that miraculous fairy, nature, and devote yourself to what lies within the realm of human conscious control.
"Put a role on the right road and it will move ahead. It will grow broader and deeper and will in the end lead to inspiration." (pp. 264–65)

The goal of acting, on stage and in life, is not perfect control of one's surroundings, not direct control of one's feelings, not inspiration or transcendent experience. The goal is simply learning to do what one can, leaving "nature" to bring about some results from the action. One gives up one's self in the doing and accepts the consequences as data for determining the next doing. On these points both Morita and Stanislavski agree. Two great thinkers with a common insight.

Treatment of a Japanese Patient

Mr. Tamura, a section chief in a manufacturing sales division, suffered from anthropophobia to the extent that he seriously considered resigning from his job. Since junior high school he had felt awkward around other people.

As a section chief it was his job to entertain business guests, make speeches, and supervise a large number of employees. Mr. Tamura lacked confidence; he had difficulty doing any of these tasks. He entered the hospital several times and had attended Moritist group therapy sessions over a number of years, with periods of relief from his problem.

During one of my trips to Tokyo he requested a therapy session with me. This would be a single meeting, so there would be no opportunity for detailed history taking and establishing rapport. I elected to bank on my authority and reputation with this fellow, condensing the therapy into a surprise-and-advise approach.

After a few minutes of listening to background material, I asked Mr. Tamura to close his eyes and describe my clothing, then to describe details of the room. With much hesitation and encouragement, he was able to do the former in general terms and the latter almost not at all. Then I asked him to open his eyes and describe the room in detail.

This first technique has several purposes. I learn the student's degree of anxiety, his willingness to follow advice, and his emphases in description. For example, does he notice objects critically? Does he focus on large objects, colorful objects, artistic objects? What can I learn from what he ignores? I explained to Mr. Tamura that, because of his superior sensitivity, he is troubled in social situations. In the future when he meets someone important to his work, or when he has to entertain a business acquaintance, he is to attend to the details of that person and the place he is in. The excess attention or awareness that previously had been turned inward on himself must from now on be turned toward the outer world. He must become an observer of details of the social and physical world in which he lives rather than an expert on the moment-by-moment changes going on within him. These inner changes are not to be denied or suppressed. Rather they are to be accepted while he devotes his awareness to the everyday reality in which he is immersed.

Next, we turned to his purposes. He wanted to quit work. Yet neither his superior at work nor his wife was willing to support this desire. Nor was I. I asked what he wished to be doing five years from now. What future did he hope for? Again, vague and general replies were not acceptable. I asked for details. Then I advised him to keep a set of notebooks with daily, weekly, and annual goals written in them. As these goals were accomplished, they were to be checked off. Those not attained in the given time period were to be added to the next if they were still important.

This log has two primary purposes. In the search for relief from symptoms the neurotic person often loses sight of his other aims and purposes in life. Writing his goals (and, if possible, reviewing them periodically with his therapist) provides a repetitive process for bringing them back to his attention and putting symptom relief into this larger life perspective. Secondly, the log provides a concrete record of successes for the person lacking in confidence. Self-confidence comes after accomplishment, not before. Many people in neurotic moments are like the student who gets a score of ninety out of a hundred on an exam and thinks only about the ten points that were missed. The student's log provides visible evidence of the ninety points earned.

After that we discussed tactics for speechmaking. I suggested techniques for making that task easier. The content of the speech in

DAVID K. REYNOLDS

the first few minutes and the last few minutes was to be memorized word for word. The rest was to be outlined and practiced several times, preferably in front of a mirror or a small audience of friends or family. When presenting his material before an audience, I advised Mr. Tamura to notice individuals in the group as much as possible and speak to them, noting their responses and interest, sitting posture, and so forth. In any case, I suggested that he seek out opportunities to speak publicly rather than trying to avoid them. At least in the beginning of treatment, it is often wise to have the student suffering from anticipatory anxiety while overpreparing for a dreaded task, provided that his preparations are in the area of realistic practice and physical effort. Merely anticipating the event is not preparation, and such anticipation only results in more anxiety. Doing something useful is far more sensible.

Mr. Tamura worried that he was a mediocre person in a position demanding too much of him. Yet he realized that he did his work well, knew more about the business than anyone else, and had more experience than anyone at his particular job. We could have spent some time exploring his notion of "mediocrity" until the analysis of his conception changed his attitude about it (perhaps by finding the concept of mediocre empty of meaning). Within our short time together, however, I recommended the more direct tactic of accepting himself, his mediocrity, his worries about mediocrity, all of it, as it is. Accept it to death. The internal struggle about not wanting to be mediocre is simply another hindrance to getting done what needs to be done. Let him get on about living life ably, and self-criticism will diminish.

Finally, I announced that he was already both a therapist and a patient, both a teacher and a student. His years of therapy had involved numerous opportunities to observe how therapists speak and act. I reminded him that many people see their lives flash before their eyes as they die. Such visions include others' responses to them, so others' behavior styles must be stored away somewhere in the mind. Mr. Tamura was instructed to make efforts to act with "a therapist's heart." That is, he was to utilize the expertise he had unwittingly gained through the years of therapy for the benefit of those around him. Rather than complain to his wife about his own troubles, he was to return home and ask about *her* problems with housework and the children and ask how *he* could help. Had there been time, we would have done role-playing, with my acting as Mr. Tamura's student.

Mr. Tamura was surprised to hear that within him was a latent therapist. He was also surprised to learn that patients "treat" therapists. That is, treating patients helps therapists with their own problems, creates confidence within the therapists themselves, and holds all sorts of additional benefits. Teachers need their students at least as much as the students need teachers.

At the end of our session the various plans and tactics were thoroughly reviewed and Mr. Tamura was asked once more to close his eyes and describe his surroundings. Of course, a much more competent description was elicited this time. The astute reader will have noticed that I asked Mr. Tamura to be a participant observer, lecturer, and therapist—all roles that I adopt at one time or another. My other students have been advised to write daily diaries of observations and activities, much like this written account. I have no particular need to create imitations of myself. Rather, I know that these tactics for playing ball on running water are helpful for the extremely sensitive person.

DAVID K. REYNOLDS

Morita's Life—"Effort Is Good Fortune"

Scholars create history and historical biography with the same impunity with which they create descriptions of preliterate cultures hidden in the jungles. In the case of Morita Shoma (in Japanese, the family name comes first), we have his diaries, a seven-volume set of collected writings, his books, and a few of his students and patients who are still alive—all these factors keep our descriptions of his life within the bounds of probable reality.

We know that Morita was a rare Japanese, less fettered by the extreme concern with propriety generally found in the middle and upper classes. He took patients into his home so that he could train them in everyday living skills. He encouraged them to ignore the usual distinctions of status. In fact, they couldn't ignore the hierarchical distinctions that order Japanese society. But to make the gesture of living as human equals was an extraordinary step for a Japanese in the early twentieth century.

When he was healthy, Morita worked in the garden alongside his patients. He taught them how to knead magazine paper for use as toilet tissue. He required that nothing that was reusable be wasted. For example, the water used in the washbasin was collected and used to mop floors; then this mop water was used on the plants outside. When the regular workman failed to show up, this noted professor of medicine donned work clothes and shoveled out the cesspool. Why engage in these menial tasks? The answer is simple: because they needed to be done.

In his waning years Morita had his nurse push him around town in a baby buggy. There were no wheelchairs; he didn't wish to be confined to his bed. Morita remained curious about the world even during the long illness that eventually led to his death. He accepted his feelings of embarrassment and hesitation as they were, and went straightforwardly ahead with his undertakings. He lived the philosophy that he taught his students and patients.

During his convalescence, many came to bring flowers and gifts —as is the custom in Japan and elsewhere. Morita saw that there were duplicates and perishable gifts going to waste. So he posted a notice at the entrance to his house listing the gifts that were acceptable to bring. The list was headed by the all-purpose gift money, but it also included rice and other household necessities. When I tell this story to Japanese friends they are shocked and amused by the temerity of this man. To attempt to regulate the sorts of gifts others bring is very nearly unthinkable. But it made good sense to Morita Shoma, and he did what he determined needed to be done.

Observational skills are well reflected in Morita's life. He noted the details of his patients' behaviors and of his own. His diaries contain notes on the number of rainy and snowy days each month, the number of visitors who came by, the times and circumstances in which he drank sake, even the number of times he had sexual intercourse each month.

DAVID K. REYNOLDS

Student Diaries

Most students/clients in Morita therapy are required to maintain daily journals. The journals are turned in each week for the therapist's comments. I have included here a couple of edited samples from such journals. The first selection is from the first week's journal of a new client. The therapist's comments are italicized in parentheses.

FEELINGS	BEHAVIOR
Monday	
Tired *(Include the exact time)*	Washing face
Tired	Sitting down with a glass of wine
Bleak	Still sitting down
Wanting to hold Elaine	Eating cheese
Scarred *(sic)*	Loss of apetite *(sic)* *(Pay attention to everything, including spelling.)* *(Loss of appetite is a feeling, not a behavior.)*
Fear	Holding stomach

Loss of Elaine—she didn't want to see me tonight	Not wanting to do anything *("Not wanting to" is not a behavior. You are always doing something—sitting, lying down, pacing are behaviors, too.)*
Loneliness	Still no appetite, tired, sleepy *(Feelings, not behavior)*
Hopeless due to fear, loss, loneliness	
Fear has passed, a bit calmer, missing Elaine, bored	Still no appetite, but ate a mango

Tuesday Morning

9:20

Stomach aches	Stayed in bed
Feeling knees, chest, arms	Hiding
Rejected, lost	

9:30

Stronger feelings *(Don't forget to include time)*	Cigarette and coffee
Work is overpowering	I must get out there and deal with the salesmen. *(Behavior is what you do, not what you think.)*
Confusion about job, stomach hurts	Calls to contractors
Happy, safer	Working

(Notice how feelings change over time. Sometimes you will feel terrific, sometimes terrible. Become the kind of person who does well under either condition.)

The next selection is from a student who had been in Morita therapy for about a month. I had asked the young man to write comments on his own journal as a Morita therapist would. His comments are in brackets. As before, my comments are italicized in parentheses.

10 A.M.

Decided to go back to sleep.

Didn't want to go to class.

Woke up to alarm.

[Get up and proceed with the day.]

11 A.M.

Optimistic, slight headache.

Felt well rested. Determined to do things right. Trying to convince myself that living life by Morita principles would be easier and give me security. Therefore eliminating by (sic, "my?"—attention!) incredible feelings of being overwhelmed. Taking things one step at a time is an important lesson for me.

Sitting down to meditate.

[Close your eyes and begin to meditate regardless of the way you are feeling.] (Do what you need to do.) (Write as much detail about behavior as you do about feelings.)

12 noon

Enjoying meal; tense; not liking how I feel physically, not liking my self-image. Wanting to strike up conversation with the woman next to me.

Eating breakfast out.

[Taste the food.]

12:40 P.M.

Looking at women in passing cars. Thinking I deserve to have one of them and make it in the real world.

Riding home from coffee shop.

1:10 P.M.

Very anxious; head spinning; maybe too much coffee. Afraid of seeing Arlene tonight.

Sinuses closed tight.

[Tight sinuses can present a new task. Take medication.]

Calling up record shop to see how late they are open.

[Good. You did what you needed to do.]

3:00 P.M.

Satisfied with myself that I took my friend, Greg, despite not feeling well. Enjoying looking at album covers. *(Lose yourself in them.)*

Looking at albums in record shop.

5:00 P.M.

Feeling physically horrible. Dizzy, afraid I was going out of my mind. Anxious; what should I do? Rest? Go out anyway?

Lying down; resting.

7:00 P.M.

Feeling much better, both physically and emotionally. Happy that Arlene "allowed" me to feel the way I felt without hassling me. Enjoying being with Arlene.

Sitting on the couch with Arlene.

10:00 P.M.

Feeling very good. Head aches but took aspirin.

Talking with Arlene.

Emotionally clear; very comfortable with Arlene.

11:30 P.M.

Delicious food; relaxed.

Eating late dinner with Arlene. Aware of ripoff prices, but accepting.

[Enjoy the meal, the company.]

(No, if you enjoy, then enjoy)

Other selections from this diary with comments follow:

5:00

Aware of weariness. Concentrating on what I am doing.

Showering. *(Good!)*

9:20

A little anxious at times.

Doing dishes.

DAVID K. REYNOLDS

[Look at what you have accomplished.]

10:30

Feeling all right. Enjoying the show. I had plan *(sic)* to allow myself this one diversion/relaxation. [Relaxation, too, can be a task at hand. Do "it"— whatever "it" is, *fully.*]

Watching *Columbo* on TV.

11:10

Legs hurt; but very satisfied at what I've done this evening. *(You earned that satisfaction. Congratulations!)* A little anxious about all the things I need to do and am avoiding. Oh, well. [No need to constantly analyze what you are anxious about. Accept your feeling and keep doing your task.]

Doing dishes.

10:00 A.M.

Annoyed at myself for being late.

Driving to class.

[Then resolve to go to bed earlier and wake up earlier.] *(No need to "resolve," just do it.)*

Other comments the client wrote to himself included:

Enjoy the good time. Remember, though, that you can't expect this feeling to be the same every time.

Do it fully. Too much analyzing can get in the way of doing the task.

Purpose!

Good! Lose yourself in what you are doing.

Feeling virtuous about accomplishments or not, watch the television show with full attention.

Lying in bed, feeling no energy, being down on myself—each implies the other. Get up!

One can be satisfied and frustrated at the same time; pay attention to the task.

Life does not always go smoothly. But we can greet it with consistency.

Continued practice will increase efficiency.

Is my purpose here to impress? Be clear on purpose.

Thinking to a point is okay . . . *but* do not let yourself ruminate without doing the next task.

As can be seen, the principles described in this book are neither difficult to understand nor difficult to remember. Within a month of weekly sessions, reading, and journals with annotations, this young man had grasped much of Morita's basic teaching. There were still misunderstandings as, for example, when he set himself the uncontrollable task of "enjoying" the meal and the company. I have the impression that his understanding of the term *task* is still somewhat puritanically narrow. Although he sees that relaxation can be a task, too, he writes as if the truly satisfying ("virtuous") tasks are those involving (disagreeable? onerous?) work. Accomplishing the task of sunbathing or daydreaming or listening to records or slicing into a chilled watermelon is as worthy as doing dishes, provided that the task is what needs to be done in that moment. Only the client knows what needs to be done in that moment.

Exercises in Living—The Ball Game

In this chapter and in the next I suggest some exercises for developing skill at playing ball on running water. These exercises are by no means trivial. They are extremely difficult when done correctly, when done with attention and with purpose. You may wonder at first why these exercises are assigned. Perhaps you will no longer wonder after you have become accomplished at them. Very few people are skillful at all of them. Very few of my clients/students are skillful at any of them when they first come for training.

The assignments are:

1. Get up in the morning.
2. Prepare breakfast.
3. Talk with someone.
4. Take a walk.
5. Clean the streets in your neighborhood.
6. Scrub your bathroom.
7. Eat dinner.
8. Play a game.
9. Take a bath or shower.
10. Go to bed.

The assignments in this program of self-development need not be carried out in any particular order. You need not master one before starting on another. There is no time limit involved, although I expect that progress can continue for months and years. Before beginning on the list, you might want to practice with the following assignment: Write a list of things that need to be done. I recommend a simple list for a start. The list should be relatively short, basic, practicable, concrete, immediate. No grand items like "put myself through college," "find the perfect woman for me and marry her," "retire in the South Pacific." The list should contain items like "write in my journal every day this week," "get up in time to eat a balanced breakfast," "mail the check for the mortgage payment," "make five phone calls today for job interviews," "do dishes immediately after dinner," "take the car in Tuesday for servicing," "read ten pages in a new book," "shave every morning this week," "write a thank-you letter to Aunt Carrie," and so forth. Include some fun things—fun things need doing, too. But what goes on the list should be determined by whether or not it needs to be done, and not on the basis of its pleasantness or disagreeableness.

Someone suggested that we should do something unpleasant every day as a sort of means of self-development—a subjugation of the ego. I'm not at all interested in that sort of thing here. I *am* very much interested in getting done what needs to be done, whether it is pleasant or not. Can you see the difference between these approaches? The other approach is focused on the discomfort or drudgery of changing the oil in the crankcase or cleaning the toilets; Morita therapy is focused simply on getting that oil changed and the toilets cleaned. The doer hardly fits into the picture at all except as a means of getting those tasks accomplished.

What a strange notion, you might think. Am I not important enough to be the center of my world? Shouldn't the pleasantness or unpleasantness of a task *to me* be the most important consideration when I undertake even some small project? I seriously doubt that anyone ignores the personal gratification or torment involved in his or her actions. But the greatest payoff comes to the individual who simply notes with attention that this necessary task is going to be interesting (or painful or frightening or exhilarating or embarrassing or some combination of feelings) and gets on about accomplishing what needs to be done.

DAVID K. REYNOLDS

Now let's take a look at the listed tasks one by one.

1. *Get up in the morning.*

As soon as you awaken in the morning, it is time to get up. The business of snooze alarms is foolishness. If you need the help of an alarm to get you awake, set it once and hold to your purpose of getting up at that time.

If you need help cutting through the habit of an early-morning debate with yourself about getting up, try reciting a poem or singing a song on awakening while you swing your legs out of bed. Get your body up and moving, all the while noticing which foot touched the floor first, what your hands are doing (rubbing your eyes, running through your hair, and so on), where your body is taking you (to the bathroom, the closet, the kitchen, and so on). Practice being alert from the moment consciousness returns each morning.

Notice which hand turns on which faucet first, how you wash, dry, wipe, dress, make the bed, and so on. Notice which arm goes into a sleeve first, which trouser leg is pulled on first, how you go about putting on socks and shoes. Let your mind and your eyes move with your actions, always with awareness, always paying attention. Life was not meant to be groped through in a fog of semi-sleep. Jump into it right from the start of the day! Don't lose even those early-morning minutes.

2. *Prepare breakfast.*

Breakfast makes more than nutritional sense. The way in which one prepares (or bolts or avoids) breakfast sets the tone for other activities during the day. Breakfast offers a first-rate clue to the precision and breadth of life lived for each of us. If you haven't put much thought into breakfast because you were too groggy or too hurried to notice what you were eating anyway, set that alarm a little earlier for a while.

Preparation for breakfast comes as you shop for those items that will make breakfast worth getting up early for. You may want to lay out some utensils or do some food preparations the night before in order to save time in the morning. Whatever you find tasty and whatever you consider good for you, a thoughtfully prepared breakfast is a morning message to your body that you value it. It is a message your body likes to receive.

Attend fully to the way you peel an orange or crack an egg. Pick up and put down the spatula with attention. Find the very best place for the teapot or the cup of coffee. Vary the spices to keep from getting bored by the same ingredients. And notice how difficult it is to keep attentive. Notice the mind wandering and bring it back to the preparation at hand or to the flavors of the food as you eat. Observe how difficult it is to put thought into preparing breakfast over and over during the week if you haven't the habit already.

The same principles apply whether you prepare breakfast for yourself or for a family or for a coffee shop full of customers. Preparing breakfast is a step in preparing yourself—for the day, for playing ball on running water.

3. Talk with someone.

The keys to constructive conversation are attentive listening and careful speaking. The words that others take the trouble to offer us as they speak deserve to be treasured. There is truth and effort behind everything that they say. It is our responsibility to practice listening carefully for the truth underlying what we hear.

Perhaps we have become desensitized by advertising on radio and television, which runs as mere background noise through our days. We have become skillful at tuning out the word gifts that are offered to us. Far too often our minds are on something else as we half listen to even the important people in our lives. Or we begin preparing our replies even before they have finished speaking. By our careful listening we can influence those around us to choose more carefully the word gifts they offer in speech. It is a rare experience to be listened to by someone who remains totally attentive. Such listening changes what we say and the way we say it.

Equally important, we need to choose carefully the words we offer those who loan us their ears. Much of what we say need not be said at all; much could be said more precisely, more humanely. This exercise of conversation involves consideration of what we can offer of ourselves to others as we speak. What is our purpose in saying that we are exhausted, that the television is too loud, that we want to be trusted more, that our companion looks radiant, that life goes on anyway? What is the truth behind the smallest utterance?

One effect of this exercise will be to slow down conversations.

DAVID K. REYNOLDS

Because others are used to talking rapidly in order to get in what they want to say, you will find that by the time you have processed some listening and some decision about what needs to be said in reply, the conversation has passed along to another subject. More often than not, you will discover that your lack of input went unnoticed and, furthermore, what you planned to say wasn't necessary after all. You will find yourself listening more of the time, and learning from even the repeated stories that you thought you had "heard" before.

You are engaged in an exchange of gifts, word gifts. All word gifts are valuable.

At one of the Morita therapy group meetings, some young people were discussing difficulties they experienced participating in conversations. They shared the common problem of sometimes finding nothing to contribute. Feeling themselves on the periphery of things, they became inattentive and unusually sleepy. They felt left out and hurt and angry at themselves for their lack of ability to break into the conversation. They searched and searched for some entry point that would seem natural, but found none. They began to feel desperate when talk flagged and they sensed that it was their turn to carry the conversational ball. I suspect that many of us have faced a similar dilemma at one time or another.

More experienced group members pointed out that sometimes conversation does flag; sometimes there is nothing particular that needs to be said. That circumstance, too, is reality; it is natural; it is all right. To view silence as a problem, a personal problem requiring me to remedy it, is a construction we lay upon the reality that is fine in and of itself.

The root of the difficulty, again, is in the self-focus of the neurotic habit of thought. We try to invent questions and conversation that will make the other person think us interesting. When our genuine purpose is to find out about the world (someone in the group, for example), a question spontaneously springs to mind. When the genuine purpose is to serve (to offer our attention and effort to others), there is no intruding self-consciousness. When we listen with full attention for the truth behind the words spoken by others, there is less likelihood of feeling sleepy or left out.

At first the young people in this group sought conversational tricks; they looked for measures that would make them appear confident and at ease in the presence of others. It is, after all, discomforting to feel left out while others seem to be enjoying an animated chat. They began to see, however, that the problem was more fundamental than a lack of skill in conversational tactics. Conversations, too, provide another occasion for observation of and losing oneself in the world. Listening, probing, laughing, picking up the coffee cup, paying the bill, replying to another's question, passing the sugar and cream —all these activities merit full attention and awareness. When these activities are done well (that is, with full attention) then the momentary discomforts of self-consciousness and lack of confidence take their places in a proper perspective.

4. Take a walk.

Walking provides an ideal pace for observing the world. The faster we go the less we see. Compare the paces of walking, bicycling, driving, and flying. Walking brings the world past my field of vision in a manner that keeps me interested without flooding my senses with exhausting speed.

Morita pointed out that our minds seem to operate as though our bodies were in motion. Our minds eagerly process information as we stroll down the street. When we sit down or lie awake for long periods, our minds seem to work just as before, but now without the stimulus input provided by walking. So our minds generate their own stimuli—for some people that means going over and over past events or creating all sorts of imaginary scenarios of future difficulties or asking unanswerable questions of themselves or daydreaming or conjuring up ideas for books. Walking, and paying attention to what one encounters, is a great help to many depressed people. They may not feel like walking—we know about the difference between feeling like doing something and actually doing it—but they need the movement and stimulus input to break into the cycle of negative thinking and inactivity.

In this exercise the walk can be taken solely for pleasure or as a trip to the market or whatever. Provided there is no medical reason to curtail it, the walk should last at least thirty minutes each day. You can vary the pace depending on your physical condition, time constraints, and other purposes. I suggest that you spend some of the time attending to the way your body moves as you walk. Notice the fluidity as the parts of your body move together in rhythm. Break the rhythm on purpose, swing your arms in the opposite direction as you stride or swing them in wider arcs to get a further appreciation of how they operate ordinarily. Try to get lost in walking, just walking. Notice your head movement, your breathing, the way your foot greets and pushes off the ground, the feel of your clothing brushing different areas of your skin, and so forth. Walking, walking, walking, walking.

Shift your attention to what is going on about you. What has the world brought for you to see and think about? What sorts of people are about? What are they wearing? What dramas are they enacting? What greenery is about? What is there to be learned from the trash that is visible? What do you notice about the details of the houses, the yards? Observe as though you were going to be quizzed in detail about what you saw. If you were my student, a quiz would be exactly what you would be expecting. Observing, observing, observing, observing.

5. Clean the streets in your neighborhood.

I am asking you to collect trash in this exercise. Haven't you ever wished that someone would pick up those blowing papers in the street or that people would be more careful about where they disposed of their bottles and cans? Haven't you ever grimaced in disgust at litter in your neighborhood? In this exercise we work on doing something about the litter while working on our egos and self-concepts at the same time.

What are people going to think about you, walking around in old clothes with a big plastic trash bag and picking up trash? Interesting that their thoughts should be such a concern. If some sheltered practice is needed, try a different neighborhood or go into the streets with a group of people on this project.

Because the exercise involves physical activity, you will find that your attention gets drawn into the work pretty readily. Keep noticing where your attention is. When you become distracted by stray thoughts and worries about what others might be thinking, remind yourself of your purpose. Your primary purpose is simply to make the world a bit cleaner. It is a purpose worthy of any of us, and you are certain to accomplish it with even a little effort. Thank you for that effort.

6. *Scrub your bathroom.*

Do this with full attention, noticing the feelings come and go. Do the task as well as you can.

7. *Eat dinner.*

The same principles of preparation should be applied to breakfast, lunch, and dinner. Slicing, stirring, pouring, washing, all need to be done attentively (mindfully) and not "automatically" or in a sloppy manner. Preparation of a meal, like any aspect of life, can be carried out artistically, gracefully. Even the most routine tasks become more interesting as you look for a thoughtful way to carry them out. Efficiency, beauty, purpose can be an integral part of any routine. Take the Japanese tea ceremony as an example and model.

Here, however, I wish to emphasize the eating aspect of dinner. No television, no book, no newspaper, no radio, nothing dedicated to distracting you from the experience of attentively eating your meal.

8. *Play a game.*

There are all sorts of purposes in playing games. Morita therapists discourage too much game playing because some people use games to escape from facing what they know that they need to take care of in their lives. But an occasional game does offer the opportunity to further train our attention, to find and hold to a purpose, to accept our feelings as they are.

Any game that requires some attention and effort to play well will do. Avoid games of pure mindless chance. Appropriate table games include chess, checkers, Scrabble, bridge, and the like. Fast-moving competitive sports such as table tennis, tennis, basketball, and volleyball are also fine. As you would expect, the quality of your play is more important than the particular game you select.

Finding a partner to play with will be a challenge to some; others already have someone in mind. When inviting someone to play, simply cling to your purpose. If you are shy and hesitate to initiate contact with another person, go right ahead and be shy—but invite someone to play anyway. If you meet refusal, immediately turn your

DAVID K. REYNOLDS

attention to what needs to be done next: inviting someone else, probably.

Work hard at keeping your mind on the game. Play purposefully with an overall plan and specific tactics. Notice the sorts of things that distract you from attending to the game in each moment. Do you think too far ahead and miss the immediate opportunity? Do you get disgusted with yourself for missing the last play and so lose the next few plays? Do minor physical discomforts intrude on your attention? Do you get annoyed and distracted by your opponent's habits? Are you intimidated into self-consciousness and a self-defeating attitude by your opponent's style? Notice these mental slips, then bring your mind immediately back to the play at hand.

Work on playing, only playing, until something more important emerges that needs to be done. And don't let the attention slip when the playing is over. Attend to winning well or losing well with full attention. Continue playing ball even when the ball game is over.

9. Take a bath or shower.

Of course, you bathe and shower all the time, but do you carry out these activities mindfully? Do you attend to the way in which you adjust the temperature of the water? Have you found the most efficient and graceful way to soap your body? Have you noticed the feel of the soap on different parts of your body? What are your feet doing? Your eyes? Your mouth? What are your purposes in bathing? How do you determine to begin, to end?

This exercise continues the extension of focused awareness to another everyday activity.

10. Go to bed.

Dr. Takehisa Kora, the noted Morita therapist mentioned above, recommends reading light nonfiction in bed before going to sleep. A novel might pull us into its contents and keep us up long hours reading. A heavy textbook might require too much attention to comprehend its meaning. Something that is neither too interesting nor too difficult, something that will inform us as we prepare for sleep—that is just what we need, Dr. Kora advises.

If you lie in bed most nights more than fifteen or twenty minutes before going to sleep, then you aren't very efficient about the sleep process. Stay up later or get up and write letters or take care of other tasks.

All of us have nights now and then when we experience difficulty getting to sleep, or we wake up and can't get back to sleep. The harder we try to make ourselves sleep, the harder it is to doze off. Sleep is another area over which our will has no direct control. Like other feelings, we must accept sleepiness and wakefulness as they are. We can use our behavior to promote the likelihood of what we want. For example, I can direct a cold breeze on my face when I am driving at night. And I can continue a regular bedtime routine to encourage drowsiness. But these actions won't guarantee successful manipulation of my feelings. Often they work; sometimes they don't. Then it is up to me to recognize the new situation and get on about doing what needs doing next.

Sleep difficulties that continue over a long time should be checked out by a physician. But unless there is some clear physical malfunction, the use of sleeping medications should be avoided. The quality of sleep is affected by soporifics and tranquilizers. Under ordinary circumstances, our bodies will see that we get satisfactory amounts of sleep provided we give them proper diet and exercise and a reasonably regulated life. Temporary sleep disturbances may be a bit annoying, but they aren't serious. Keep on about daily activities whether you sleep well or not. Your body will take care of the rest.

DAVID K. REYNOLDS

Advanced Exercises

The preceding exercises dealt with basic, everyday activities. They need to be carried out properly in order to build a solid foundation for other aspects of living. The following ten exercises may not all be appropriate for your circumstances. By now, the reasons for each exercise should be pretty clear to you. And the manner in which each exercise should be carried out should be apparent. This matter of living constructively isn't complicated or difficult to understand, although it requires attention to detail and a great deal of effort. Here are the advanced exercises:

1. Dig, plant, and care for a garden.
2. Volunteer some of your time in a nursing home.
3. Write a journal of the sounds you hear.
4. Analyze the psychological advice in television shows.
5. Read and compare the writings of Sheldon Kopp, Fritz Perls, Constantin Stanislavski, and Dogen.
6. Consider where meditation fits into playing ball.
7. Give away something you value to someone who can't repay you.
8. Give a name to a feeling that you have experienced, a feeling that has no name in English.
9. Keep a journal about what you have received from others, what you have returned to them, and what troubles you have caused them during that day.

10. Explain the principles of playing ball on running water to someone else, giving examples from your life.

Briefly, the first exercise demonstrates the literal fruits of effort and waiting. The second exercise is practice in making the time to give yourself away. The third exercise develops more attentiveness to what reality is presenting to your sense of hearing. Remember, you must notice what reality is bringing you in order to know what needs to be done. The fourth exercise helps you become more aware of the sorts of information and misinformation we are presented daily in dramas and comedies on television. Notice particularly the messages about trying to control feelings and the messages about irresponsibility for behavior because of strong feelings. These television messages are contrary to what you have been reading in this book; I submit that they are contrary to your experience also.

Exercise five asks you to look at four writers from different cultures who offer similar insights. Note how their views are similar and how they are different. Are they "playing ball" by the same rules? Exercise six is another way of asking what the difference is between attending fully to quiet sitting and attending fully to putting away the groceries. Exercise seven involves more than abandoning some valued object. Exercise eight is a reminder that feelings are not ignored in this lifeway. Feelings are worth our careful attention, too. But they must not be allowed to become an obsession, and they must not be allowed to determine what we do.

Exercise nine is borrowed from another lifeway therapy called Naikan (a word meaning "inside looking" or "introspection" in Japanese). It provides a good supplement to the views of Morita therapy in that it helps us remember in detail the ways in which we take and take from the world without repayment or gratitude or even recognizing the many ways in which we take. (For more information about the Naikan lifeway, you may want to read my book *Naikan Psychotherapy*.)

Finally, explaining ideas to someone else is a fine, active way of making sure that I understand the ideas myself. It is often said, and true in my experience, that we learn more by teaching than our students ever learn from us.

PART II

MORITIST FAIRY TALES

AND ALLEGORIES

Introduction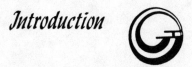

In my practice of Moritist education I sometimes find it useful to create a story for a particular student. The story is designed to touch on issues of importance in the student's life. Consideration of a fairy tale sometimes gives the perspective and distance that eases the student's confrontation with the ways he or she avoids accepting reality as it is. The stories provide an occasion and vehicle for our talking about aging, about the common propensity for trying to impress others, about revealing our imperfections, about recognizing anger, about playing the role of passive victim, about creating hope, and so forth. Included here are several of these stories, along with brief discussions of some of the issues they raise.

The Elevator

I dreamed last night that several of us had been placed in a huge mansion or temple high on an isolated rock spire. There was an elevator, which would allow us to descend to safety if we could only find and activate it. Certainly, we had been transported into this labyrinth of rooms by the same elevator. We needed only to discover it among the myriads of secret passages, sliding walls, and other disguised structural features of the building.

As we searched, Zen monks and nuns wandered about the building, going about their business. Apparently, they knew the location of the elevator, but they were silent, requiring us to find it for ourselves. Someone opened the door to a room in which a handful of Buddhist priests was chanting. He stood fascinated in the doorway until I pulled him away to continue our search. The elevator couldn't be found by listening for a clue from the chants—they were only a distraction.

A short hallway connected two large rooms. We felt along the walls of the rooms for some spring that would set them in motion downward. There seemed to be vertical traverses along which these rooms might move. But we were having no luck in putting them in motion. Suddenly, it dawned on me that the connecting hallway might be the elevator and not one of the rooms themselves. While the others went off elsewhere, a few students and I stood in the hallway, closed the doors to the adjoining rooms, and searched for some hidden lever or button. In a few seconds the hallway began to descend, and we emerged safely at the base of the mountain.

We noticed that the elevator didn't ascend again after it had discharged us. Rather another "hallway-elevator" began to lift a few rooms away. When the remaining students returned to the hallway and found us gone, they would try to descend as we had but would discover that the hallway we had used was no longer an elevator. It would require of them another imaginative step to realize that the elevator had shifted to another hallway. Still, they had the clue that the hallways might provide the movement, if they could only break free of the obsession that it was *this particular* hallway, just as we had broken free of the obsession that a room must be the elevator and hallways were merely passages between them.

As I tell this allegory to my student, I am reminded that during a period of research in nursing homes and hospital wards for the long-term and terminally ill, I was surprised to see the halls of the wards used by patients for sitting and socializing even more than the dayrooms provided for that purpose. The hallways were more than passages from room to room; they were social spaces where action and interaction flourished. Those well enough to get into chairs or wheelchairs came out of their rooms to find out what was happening in the ward world. Architects would do well to consider such a function when designing health-care facilities.

We sometimes think of life as movement from job to job or place to place or from home to the market or from the kitchen to the sofa. We put our minds in the next room and fail to notice the passageway. We are so intent upon making our appointment on time that we fail to live fully during our driving on the way to the appointment. Rooms of life sometimes disappoint us after we have entered them and have explored their potential to get us where we thought we wanted to go. Let's not neglect the hallways of living.

The Frog Prince

Once upon a time there was a prince who had been turned into a frog. The transition wasn't instantaneous as is the fate of most prince-frogs; in this case the process was gradual, over thirty years or so. You would think that a gradual change might be less traumatic than a sudden transformation; the royal fellow had a chance to adjust to his amphibian status. But, in a way, the slow change was even worse. The inevitability of the final result ate away at the prince's mind. Day by day he noticed that his voice was changing, warts were appearing, his skin color was becoming gray-green, his eyes and feet and back were turning froglike, and he was shrinking in size.

That's not an experience likely to produce gusto in a prince.

"What's happening to me? What witch have I offended to produce this spell of hoppititis?" he wondered.

The prince spent a few years flitting around the land getting kisses from princesses before he turned completely "froginous" and ugly. After all, he had read the traditional stories about the magic antidote of a maiden's kiss. Unfortunately, the virus strain that he suffered from didn't respond to the magic of that old wives' tale. Eventually, he gave up and accepted his gradual transformation.

To make a long "tale" short (after all, that is how tadpoles become frogs), by age sixty the prince was a complete frog, hopping along, minding his diet, completely resigned to his "frogosity."

He fell in love with an elderly lady frog and, upon kissing her warty, fly-specked face, he found that he was instantly changed into a temporary prince again. From then on, for varying periods of time after kissing her he felt as if he were a prince and she were a princess. How about that!

This story, of course, is about growing old. It was written for a middle-aged man who was beginning to recognize his mortality and the irreversibility of his aging. He had begun searching for the magical maiden's kiss, a cause of some consternation in his family. The humor provided some additional distance from the immediacy of his age-related anxiety. The story provided the occasion for thought and discussion about the reality that princes grow old; that is, if they live long enough, all princes become frogs.

Indian Maiden

Once upon a time there was an Indian maiden named Bright Eyes. Some people of the tribe said that she got her name from the tears that sparkled in her eyes. Others said that her eyes looked bright because she looked with intelligence and wonder at all around her. Bright Eyes had a pet falcon named Claw. This is the story of Bright Eyes and her strange pet.

One day as the young maiden walked through the forest gathering berries, she chanced upon a wounded bird. It was running and flapping in a circle around and around, dragging its broken wing and snapping viciously at everything in sight. Bright Eyes was appalled at the sharp temper of this winged beast. This falcon wasn't aloof and in control of itself like the soaring eagle. It was nasty, brutish, foul-tempered.

"How ugly it looks," she said to herself. "It is hurt, mean, and not caring who sees its display of uncivilized misbehavior." Although she winced at the savagery of the falcon, she took a liking to its courage and unselfconsciousness—this dust-covered, feather-ruffled bird of prey knocked from its sky-hunt by a warrior's misdirected arrow. She watched fascinated as it lunged and spit and fluttered furiously until helplessly exhausted from its struggles.

Bright Eyes was a kind maiden. She felt sorry for the wounded creature. She approached it and put out a hand to soothe it, only to receive a sharp peck for her trouble. She pulled back her hand and pressed some grass against the trickle of blood from her finger. She had learned her first lesson from the bird. It didn't respond directly to a reasonable, civilized approach. More careful the second time, she dropped her berry basket over the wounded bird. Then she quickly turned the basket over and lashed down the lid. She hid the basket in a small clearing near the village. As she walked back to her family's skin-covered lodge, she had already decided on the pet's name. It would be "Claw."

Within a few days she had transferred her pet to a sturdy wicker cage. Carefully, carefully. Bright Eyes had decided—she didn't know just when this decision had been made—to keep her Claw outside of the village. Somehow he didn't seem to fit in that civilized place, in that society of humans. He was too temperamental, too emotional, too uncontrollable.

She fed the falcon with pieces of meat taken from the cooking fires of her family and lovers. When the falcon ate, its energy revived and it thrashed about in its cage, trying to escape. Its frenzy resulted in other minor injuries to itself. Bloody patches showed through where the feathers had been torn off by its wild, violent eruptions. Bright Eyes watched these explosions with sorrowful fascination. Yet somehow it seemed important to Bright Eyes to keep the falcon properly penned up and not to let it go free. This impulse seemed related to the decision to keep others in the village from seeing Claw. Everything has its proper place. *A tribal maiden should be more sedate and self-contained,* she reflected. *What would others think of me if they were to find out about my wild pet?* In a sense she feared revealing her special interest in Claw to others because, at bottom, she thought there was something perverse about it. *There must be something wrong with me for keeping such a pet,* she thought.

She wished that Claw were more tame, more presentable. She even spent hours daydreaming that Claw was a meadowlark or a bluejay, prettier and better behaved. *If only my pet were well mannered, polite, obedient, I could show him to others.* There were dogs in the village that came when called, rolled over on command, even slept nestled on the blankets of their masters. But Claw retained his uncontrollable nature even after months in the cage.

In Bright Eyes's imagination Claw was the sort of creature a young brave or grizzled war chief might keep and display proudly to the village. But an Indian maiden? Yet her obsession with Claw didn't let up. She spent more time with the bird on some days than on others, but every day she found herself drawn to the secret clearing to spend time with her pet. As the months passed, Bright Eyes began to recognize that this creature, born and reared in the wilds, would never become a tame hunting falcon like the one in the village over the mountain. It would always fight to free itself, to pierce and tear at its prey, to soar and plunge, to struggle and snap. Its sharp, wicked eyes were glassed over by exhaustion and pain, but only temporarily. It always wanted something beyond what it was given; it was insatiable.

Thoughts of Claw drifted into Bright Eyes's mind at all times of the day. She sewed a beaded falcon pattern on the back of her buckskin jacket. On some nights she wore the jacket to bed and lay rigid and uncomfortable because the beads pressed into her back as she thought of her Claw. The girl resisted marriage for several years because of her pet. True, she engaged in the usual liaisons in grassy glades with young men from the village. But she dreaded the reality of marriage because her husband might discover the secret of her pet falcon. To live so long with one man would provide too many opportunities for her hidden obsession to be revealed.

Her absorption in the antics of her pet caused Bright Eyes to seek out all the lore about falcons. She consulted with wise old men in the tribe about the birds' habits. What did they like to eat? How did they nest? How high up in the trees did they rear their young? What sorts of cages were best to hold them? What could be done to make them more peaceful? Some of the tribal elders wondered at her interest in such matters, but a few heard of her daily disappearances and suspected what she was about. Yet they told no one else of their suspicions. In time she would handle her situation as befitting a member of their tribe, they assured themselves.

Finally, Bright Eyes went to a shaman who advised her that the attempts to tame Claw were hopeless, that there was nothing wrong with Claw at all, that he was just fine as he was. The cage, she was

DAVID K. REYNOLDS

told, was not only unnecessary but harmful to both Claw and to Bright Eyes herself. The shaman offered her some powerful word spells and advised her to stop trying to make Claw into something that he wasn't.

It was a magical day when Bright Eyes struggled under the weight of Claw in his cage all the way to the door of the shaman's skin-covered tent near the center of the village. She quietly announced to all who had gathered around this strange sight that she had been hiding this bird of prey from others because she had thought it needed to be controlled before it would be presentable. However, she now realized that Claw was all right just as he was, without being washed or perfumed or powdered or decorated with beads. Bright Eyes opened the cage and, half fearfully, watched as her bird hopped forward to perch cautiously on the opened door. Then Claw leaped for the sky.

What happened next was most remarkable to behold. An amazed Bright Eyes saw the dwindling dot grow larger again as Claw circled and sank toward the maiden. She stood in shocked silence as the wings spread at the last moment and Claw landed on her shoulder. The claws dug through the buckskin jacket into her shoulder for a moment, but the pain was slight. Claw sat there peacefully with an eye cocked to see what Bright Eyes would do. She had the impulse to try to get him back into the cage while she had the chance. Still, she knew that such an attempt would fail, and the attempt itself would ruin everything. She let Claw sit there until he hurtled into the air again as everyone watched.

As the bird took off, the claws released her shoulder but ripped across the beaded pattern sewn into the back of her jacket. The beads scattered to the ground. Bright Eyes gazed with mixed feelings at the soaring falcon. Deep inside she knew that she had done the right thing in releasing Claw, in allowing the bird to climb into its airy freedom. She felt some puzzlement, too, that her feet stayed firmly on the ground. It was almost as if she had expected to be swept off her feet with the rush of Claw's wings. Yet all she felt was an inner lightness from the moment the cage door was opened.

Claw was in his element now. How different he looked in the

lofty distance riding the currents of air. After a few moments Bright Eyes turned her eyes back to the earth and walked off to gather wood for the evening cooking fire.

This tale was written for a civilized young woman who avoided accepting all of her feelings as they were. In particular, she had trouble looking at her moments of rage and despair. Like Claw, her primitive feelings were unworthy of being recognized or displayed to others, she thought. She hid them well, although they manifested themselves in back spasms and other symptoms. Rage isn't pleasant to experience, but it will not sweep us from our feet when we are firmly planted on the ground of self-guided behavior.

On Trusting

Millie had an unusual way of painting with watercolors. Her fourth-grade teacher noticed that Millie never let the colors mix together—not on the paint tray, not on the brush (she washed it out carefully before beginning on a new color), and, most of all, not on her paper as she painted. If Mille painted a man, he was all yellow or all white or all black or all brown. His skin, shirt, hair, shoes and pants were all the same color.

Her trees all had green trunks if they had green leaves. Her blue skies had blue clouds. Her brick red houses had red doors, and so on.

Furthermore, around each object in her painting was an outline of unpainted space. The blue sky never actually touched the red brick house. The brown man was slightly separated from his yellow umbrella. Like that.

Millie's teacher wondered why her pupil kept everything apart in her pictures. So she asked about it.

"It's better that way," Millie told her simply.

"Why is it better?"

"It just is."

This line of questioning is going nowhere, thought the teacher. *I'll try from a different angle.*

"What would happen if the colors mixed on your painting? What if the blue sky and the green tree touched?" she asked.

"It would get ugly . . . I think," replied the girl after some thought. "I'm not really sure what would happen."

"Look at this picture." The teacher held up another child's watercolor painting. "Isn't it pretty the way the color of her flowers mixed together here? See the beautiful fuzziness of the white and gray clouds in the blue sky?"

"That's Leah's painting, not mine."

"But yours could look like this, too."

"Maybe. I'm not sure. Things get too close and they get mixed together and who knows what will happen? Jerry mixed a lot of colors together the other day and he got an ugly, ugly gray-brown. Like dirty dishwater."

That was the longest speech her teacher had ever heard from Millie. The words had started slowly, then they tumbled out at the end.

"I see. Would you like to try just putting a couple of colors together while I sit here and watch? Just to see what would happen?"

Millie loved her teacher, so she gave it a try.

In time she learned to mix different hues to find out which ones made beautiful contrasts and blends and which ones made muddy results.

And after more time passed she learned to appreciate which muddy combinations were dynamic and which were dead.

That's art for you.

Some people try to keep parts of their life separate from other parts. They try to keep their family life separate from their work life, their religious life separate from their leisure life, and so on. One of my patients had two sets of friends. She always gave two parties, one party for her work friends and one party for her family friends. She was afraid to invite all her friends to one party. She didn't know what would happen if all her friends met each other. This story was written for her.

We don't always know what will happen when we try something new. Some people try to assess all the angles in their minds without checking out ideas against reality through action. Like Millie in the story, we may fear new combinations in life. When there is someone we love and trust to help us, such as Millie's teacher, it is easier to take more risks in life. New combinations may be risky, but they make life more interesting.

DAVID K. REYNOLDS

Sleeping Sickness

Once upon a time there was a land in which the people thought that by sleeping with each other they could get their partners' magical powers and avoid loneliness.

They were wrong.

This is the shortest of the stories I have written for my students. It was written for a person who used seduction to bring about temporary feelings of security and to hide from gnawing loneliness. We discussed alternative activities to achieve more controllable, long-term goals.

Poor Li'l Ugly Ol' Me

All of the paintings of all of the women throughout the castle showed lovely, flawless images of beauty. But Maiden Mildred wasn't beautiful or even pretty. She was lumpy, plump; with a square face, thin, stringy hair, and pimples. She hated herself.

She also hated her mother for having a baby as ugly as she, and she hated the other maidens for looking prettier than she, and she hated me for writing about her. Oh yes, she hated the young knights, too, because they foolishly fawned over the prettiest maidens and left her sitting alone at the palace balls. Maid Mildred hated much of life. She felt miserable. Her misery and hate twisted her face into a dark scowl so that she looked even homelier than nature had made her.

A few days before Maid Mildred's twenty-ninth birthday, a blind musician came to play his lute for the court. Maid Mildred sat entranced by the ballads he sang. He showed her the sightless beauty within his music. Maid Mildred thought, *At last a man has come whose beauty I can appreciate without spoiling it by my own ugliness. He cannot see my face. I'll never allow him to touch me and discover my imperfection.*

She had the musician held in a darkened room of the castle. There she met with him every day, striving to make their meetings only the meeting of sounds. She couldn't see his face because of the dimmed lights. He couldn't see hers, of course, because of his blindness. They never touched. They sat for hours talking, and he sang and played his lute for her appreciative ears.

Maid Mildred spent more and more time in the sightless room. Her presence stimulated the musician's finest performances. But he seemed to be wasting away, exhausted by the attention and the intensity of their lightless contact.

Within six months he was dead, silent. And Maid Mildred was blind. Her eyes had grown accustomed to the dark and could not stand the light of day. The smallest candle brought instant tears and a severe headache. She never left the darkened room for the rest of her life. It is said that within the casket her face was serene and strikingly beautiful. Yet no one knew of this marvelous transformation of her features before the funeral, not even Maid Mildred.

This tale, along with the next story, concerns the struggles of my students with imperfection and perfection, with ugliness and beauty. Note that Maid Mildred set up her life situation in such a way that even when change took place she wouldn't be aware of it.

Aiming Too Low

Many years ago there was a beautiful young princess. Her father, the king, gave her everything she wanted. She dressed in the finest clothes, went to the finest school, ate the finest food, lived in the finest rooms of the palace.

At school no one knew she was a princess. Nevertheless, because of her beauty and poise, everyone treated her especially well. The teachers smiled at her and gave her first chance at answering their questions. The boys fell in love with her at first sight. Even the other girls were friendly and harbored no envy because they realized that she wasn't competing with them for the boys. She was in a class by herself.

Despite these ideal circumstances, the princess was lonely. She couldn't tell anyone how badly she felt because everyone expected her to be perfect. Even if she hinted at the isolation of her flawlessness, the people around her would have thought that she was joking. After all, she had hobbies, friends, a good family, and wealth. The princess, let us call her Hiroko, came to hate her own beauty and perfection. She saw it as a barrier between her and other people, between truth and facade, between genuine happiness and superficial happiness, between what was real and what ought to be real.

However, Hiroko was not a foolish young princess. She knew that her beauty and carriage gave her many advantages in life. So whatever course she would take to remedy her life dilemma, she would not consider making her face ugly or ruining her perfectly proportioned body.

She thought that if she could make herself ugly inside, where the ugliness wouldn't be obvious to everyone, she would feel closer to the ordinary people around her. With great deliberation and care, she went about doing all the things that might make her feel disfigured inside. She behaved in disgusting, mean, boring, meaningless ways. I'll remind you that Hiroko didn't do what she did because the people around her forced her to do them. These hurtful acts weren't the necessary price demanded by her schoolmates for joining their group. Hiroko *wanted* to act in these terrible ways. She tried to find uglier and uglier habits in order to change herself into what she wanted to become. She wanted to become more ordinary, but without risking her outer beauty.

At first, her strategy seemed to bring about the results she had expected it would. She began to feel her inner imperfection grow. She began to sense a growing separation between what she looked like on the outside and what she knew was happening on the inside. But these changes didn't make Princess Hiroko more like her schoolmates at all. The growing flaws in her character seemed to distance her even more from the normal social life of the school for the aristocracy. The boys admired her from a distance, but they feared her sudden shifts of mood and malicious tricks.

Like a flower closing itself for the evening, Hiroko began to hide her beauty. She became shy and afraid to leave her rooms in the palace. She played for hours with dolls that she hadn't touched for years. She began reading long novels to pass the days. She felt so very miserable.

It took a long time for Princess Hiroko to learn that being ordinary doesn't mean being ugly.

This story is a fictionalized version of part of the story of a young woman who came for Morita guidance. She had become the victim of her beauty rather like the maiden in the previous story had become the victim of her homeliness. The dimension of physical appearance requires particular sensitivity in our culture, it seems. But beauty here is also a metaphor for whatever sets us apart from others —athletic prowess, intelligence, wealth, stature, ethnicity, religious belief, and so forth. Being different as individuals, we search for our commonality with others, too.

DAVID K. REYNOLDS

Royalty

Once upon a time there was a prince who liked being just a prince. He knew that someday his father would step down and he would ascend to the throne, but he dreaded that day.

"I am a mere prince, Father. I have many sisters. Let one of them rule the land."

"The people expect you to rule them, my son. Why do you struggle with your destiny?"

"I am a very good prince," the young man answered. "I am skilled at doing princely things. I can hold my own in combat, woo pretty maidens, dance until dawn, and drink and ride my stallion with the best of them. But I am not a king. A king must be serious and wise and just. Kings know much more than I do. I cannot be a king."

The royal monarch only laughed.

Now it happened that later that year the ruler of the land fell ill. The illness lingered for months. It was rumored that the king was about to turn over power to his son.

The prince began to panic. "I'm not ready for this," he cried. "Can someone else take over for a few years? How about a council of governors? If only Mother hadn't died—a queen could rule the land. Oh, dear me, what shall I do?"

Two days before the coronation ceremony all the palace was in an uproar. The prince had locked himself in his room, and he refused to come out. Upon hearing this tragic news, the king immediately called the grand wizard to his sickbed. He looked the old man straight in the eye and told him to take care of the problem. The grand wizard nodded and left with a swirl of his robes. He knew exactly what to do. For hadn't a very similar event occurred forty years before, as the current monarch ascended the throne?

The grand wizard knocked on the prince's door. He carried a tray of food in his left hand.

"Go away," a voice called from inside the room.

"Sire, I have your meal tray."

"I don't want anything to eat. Go away!"

"But, Sire, I have the dynastic pill for you to take with your meal."

"The dynastic pill?" The voice sounded somewhat closer to the door.

"Of course, it is the medicine that makes you a ruler." The voice of the grand wizard was scarcely a whisper now. "You cannot reign without taking the dynastic pill."

"'I never heard of such a thing."

"And please, Sire, do not tell anyone else about it," whispered the old man. "If word got out, many would desire to take the pill and become a monarch."

Curiosity and hope filled the young man. He opened the door a crack and peeked out into the hall.

"Come in, quickly!"

The grand wizard scurried into the prince's chambers, tray in hand.

"All right, where is the pill?" demanded the prince.

"It is inside the bottle there in the center of your tray. You had best read the label and instructions carefully before taking it."

"You may go now." The prince turned away and sat on the bed with the magic bottle in his hand.

"Yes, Sire." And the grand wizard left the room.

The prince eagerly read the label on the bottle. It read: "Dynastic pill. Prepared personally by each monarch for his royal successor. Read the instructions inside carefully."

The prince pulled the glass stopper from the bottle and peered inside. A sheet of paper and one large white pill greeted his eye. *The sheet of paper must contain the instructions,* he thought.

As he began to unfurl it, his imagination turned toward the coronation banquet. In his mind's eye he pictured himself standing regally at the table head, toasting the kingdom. Poised, confident, fully a king . . .

Two days later the coronation took place without incident. The court was buzzing about the fine bearing of the new king. The common folk rejoiced at the prospect of another in a long line of wise and charismatic monarchs.

Oh yes, about the pill. As the prince's trembling fingers unfolded the instructions, he recognized his father's handwriting:

> For you, my son,
> No man is ever ready for such authority as this. No man begins by feeling like a king. You become a king by being one. In time, you will wear your crown as comfortably as anyone has.
> There is no magic in this pill. It is made of the bitterest herbs. The instructions are to hold it in your mouth until you grow used to the bitterness. Then, when you have conquered it, when the pill has completely dissolved, you may swallow it. That is all.
>
> Your loving father

Sometimes we do not feel confident to do the tasks that life brings us to do. Other people appear to be confident as they do their tasks. We want a magic pill (or an education, or a secure job, or a fine spouse, or much money, or something else) to give us confidence. But confidence comes *after* we have done our work and succeeded, not before. It is natural to lack confidence before starting a new school subject or moving into marriage or taking on new responsibilities at work. Accept the bitter taste of self-doubt while going about mastering the situation.

Stoptime

Little Suzy was in kindergarten. One day she brought a pumpkin seed home from class. Her homework assignment was to plant the seed and water it and grow a pumpkin for next Halloween.

She packed rich, black soil into a glass jar, planted her seed, watered it carefully, and set it on the kitchen window shelf. Then she sat down to watch the seed grow.

"What are you doing, Suzy?" her teen-aged sister, Lucy, asked.

"I'm waiting for the pumpkin to grow so that I can put it in a larger jar," Suzy replied.

"Silly," Lucy laughed. "It will take a long time before that pumpkin comes up."

"That's all right; I'll wait. What are you doing sitting by the phone?"

"I'm hoping Bill will call me. He's that cute new guy at school. I think he likes me."

"Does he know our phone number?" Suzy asked a sensible question.

"Hmmm. Maybe. He knows Bob, and Bob knows it."

"Oh."

Just then their father entered the kitchen.

"Any telephone calls for me, Lucy?" he asked.

"No, not this morning. Anything special?"

"Well, I sent that manuscript off to the publisher's last week. They should let me know soon if they want to handle it or not."

"Well, nothing so far."

"Thanks, I'd better get back to that lawnmower." He grabbed a can of beer from the refrigerator and went back out through the screen door.

From the next room Lucy's mother's voice could barely be heard above the whir of the sewing machine. She was talking to herself.

"When will that man come to his senses about the writing business? He could be making a good, steady living as an engineer. I've waited sixteen years for the light to dawn on him that he'll never make it as an author. If it weren't for my sewing and his parents' money . . ."

The cat scratched at the screen door. Suzy ran to let it in. Tail in the air, her chubby pet headed for the cupboard where the cat food was kept. It sat and scratched and whined in its cat's voice, waiting to be fed.

This story seems to be getting nowhere, the author thought. Perhaps tomorrow I'll think of an inspiring ending.

In this story everyone is waiting for something. Suzy is waiting for the pumpkin seed to grow; Lucy is waiting for a telephone call; the cat is waiting to be fed; even the author is waiting to finish the story. Some people seem to turn their lives off as they wait for something. In other words, they only wait and do not use their time wisely while waiting. When my younger students are waiting to learn the results of entrance examinations, when they are waiting for their bus to arrive, when they are waiting for a friend to telephone, what do they do? Life seems very long to young people, but it is too short to waste even a minute. Young or old, we recommend to our students that they fill their waiting moments with fun and study and other activity. One of our Moritist maxims is, "Don't put your life on hold."

Walls

Centuries ago in a far-off land two glumps lived in the bottom of a deep ravine that wound for hundreds of miles through the countryside. One glump was forever unhappy. He would cock his eye uneasily at the steep sides of the ravine and complain that he felt suffocated by their looming presence.

"Someday they'll tumble in on us and we'll be crushed," he growled.

"Perhaps so," replied the other glump evenly. "In the meantime we lead a pretty good life."

"Good life? How can you call this a good life? Those oppressive walls tower over us every day of our lives. I feel like an ant pressed between bookends."

"But consider our home *lengthwise*. We can travel for miles and miles, even beyond the farthest we desire to go, when we pick the wild garbles near Fern Spring."

"Who knows when a landslide might block our path? Moreover, we walk always with the walls above us," grumbled the glump.

"Yes, and always with the space ahead and behind, too."

This is a brief tale about limits and perspectives. I use it with some elderly students, handicapped students, and others who see walls (real or imaginary) looming above them. It provides the opportunity for thinking about what is possible and about the direction in which hope lies.

Pain and a Princess

Once there was a lovely young princess who was frightened by life.

I am so sensitive, she thought to herself, *life can only hurt me.* So she decided to go to bed and stay there.

The king was worried about his fragile daughter. She would soon be near the age for marriage, but who would marry such a delicate maiden?

For weeks she remained in bed most of the time, reading and eating from the trays brought to her. She refused to set foot outside her chambers.

"The world is filled with ugliness and poverty. Within my chambers I can create a world of perfection. There is no pain here, only a shade of sorrow," she told her mother.

The servants who brought her food and linens felt the aura of melancholy as soon as they entered the princess's room. She scarcely looked at them for fear of noting some worry on their brows. Recognizing others' worries would bring pain to her own heart. She worked so hard at protecting herself.

The king and queen assembled a host of advisers. Nevertheless, despite the potions and lectures and tears and commands, the princess refused to leave her room. Little by little her fairness turned into pallor, her delicate features began to look sickly, weak.

The king offered a huge reward to any nobleman who could win the heart of the princess and lure her from her chambers. Though several tried, they were soon turned back by her shy reluctance to involve herself with anyone.

"If I give myself to you, you might leave me later on. In any case you and I shall someday die, so the pain of separation is the inevitable result of love. Here I am safe, though sad." With these words she turned her head to the pillow and refused even to look again at her suitors.

One day the court physician was going to be attending a convention outside the kingdom at the time of the weekly health examination of the princess. He sent his apprentice instead.

The young physician-in-training was a serious and bright fellow. After taking the princess's pulse and examining her eyes and the color and coolness of her hands, he asked her how she was feeling.

"Neither well nor unwell," was her vague reply.

"Is there something you need? Can I get you anything?" he asked.

"No, only answer a question for me."

"Of course."

"How can you bear to see all the illness and pain your profession forces upon you? I could never endure to see the human suffering you must face every day."

The young man paused. "I do see people hurting every day. I suppose it is bearable because I try to do something about their suffering. If I just stood back and observed it and did nothing to try to help, then the effect on me would be disastrous."

"But sometimes your patient worsens and dies."

"Yes, that is true."

"Then you must know their agony and your failure, too."

"Yes. I didn't say that I help people. I said that I *try* to help people. Sometimes the results are successful; sometimes not. Sometimes my attempts seem to make my patients worse. Sometimes they get well without any help from me at all. There are many things I don't understand. It is the trying that is important somehow."

"Thank you," said the princess. She pulled the bedcovers up around her shoulders. There was much to think about.

It is unfortunate that the world won't let a princess become a nurse. For that is exactly what our princess decided she wanted most to become, or perhaps a doctor. And it is unfortunate that being of royal lineage she wasn't permitted to marry a mere physician's apprentice. After all, her affection may have been founded only upon gratitude for his saving words.

However, she left her room and, little by little, forced herself to face the pain of the world in order to work toward alleviating it. Dedicated purpose overcame her self-centeredness. And though she winced at others' pain, she carried their pain toward relief as best she could.

Some people are very sensitive to pain—their own and the pain of others. This story was written for such people. People with this sensitivity may spend a great deal of time in their rooms reading and watching television. The real world contains suffering and ugliness as well as joy and beauty. Such people prefer to pretend that the world is ideal and perfect. At least they can control the imperfection to some degree by switching channels on television and skipping pages in their books when they retreat to their rooms. The princess in this story couldn't understand how someone else could bear to face the surrounding misery of life. The young physician's apprentice suggested a way that some people have found useful. Anguish becomes more bearable when we know that we are doing all that we can to relieve constructively the conditions that cause the anguish. Sometimes, in our efforts to improve life conditions, we lose ourselves in our work. Then there is no suffering in that moment, only dedicated effort and directed attention.

A Boy and His Cat

There was once a little boy with a pet cat. He kept the cat in a wire cage all of the time. Even when he fed the cat and when he petted it, he never took the animal from its cage.

"You can't trust cats," he said. "They will run away if you give them a chance."

"But don't you love your cat?" his friend asked him.

"Not particularly," he replied. "But it's mine, and it's not going to get away."

His mother argued that since he fed the cat and stroked its furry body, the pet would want to stay nearby. But he didn't care to take any chances.

His father felt sorry for the cat and threatened to put his son in a cage so he could see what it felt like to be cooped up all the time. But the boy knew that his father was only bluffing.

Month after month passed, and the cat's restlessness turned to lethargy. The pacing stopped and the animal lay curled in a corner of the small cage day after day, refusing to eat.

"Your cat will die," his mother warned.

"Let the cat out," his father ordered.

"It's only trying to make me take it out of the cage," cried the boy, and he threw a tantrum.

So the cat stayed as it was until one day it died.

"I don't care if I take it out now," he said calmly, and he turned the cage on end and dumped the stiff, furry body into the trash. "It never got out until I was ready."

The main theme of this story concerns possessiveness. What is the relationship between love and control? This tale is useful for some troubled marriages and other relationships. As in all these fables there are subthemes that can be useful for certain sorts of clients. What does my student see as the proper child-rearing functions of parents? What part does the cat play in the permanent caging?

The Royal Prisoner

Many, many years ago a beautiful princess lived alone in the forest in a jail that she had built with her own delicate hands. The walls of the jail were made of clay, the roof was of thatch, and the door and barred windows were of wood. It had taken fifteen precious years of the princess's childhood and adolescence to construct her private prison.

Even more strange, she didn't know why she had built it at all. It had seemed a natural thing to do at the time. The castle in which her family lived was on the edge of the forest. She used to skip happily beneath the trees playing hide-and-seek with the chipmunks and robins. Perhaps the jail started as a dollhouse or a playhouse of some sort. But as she grew older the structure became bigger and more elaborate. The change from playhouse to prison was a gradual one. She found herself scraping sticks one day to make bars for the windows.

During her teen-age days the princess began spending weekends in the prison. When her formal education in the palace was completed, she moved permanently into the jail. Her friends and family at first tried to coax her out of confinement back to the castle, but she remained firm in holding to her self-imposed isolation. She seemed like some funny-sad nonreligious nun sitting alone on the bench, talking with her visitors through the barred windows. In time the visitors were fewer and fewer. At last, the king sent a servant with her meals and fresh clothing each day—that daily visit represented her only contact with the castle.

In truth, the princess left her little prison daily to take a short stroll under the trees by herself. She also kept a small garden, just enough for an occasional fresh vegetable and spice. It was a peaceful though confining existence. While living thus, she waited. She wasn't sure what she was waiting for, but she waited. Sometimes patiently, sometimes impatiently she waited in her prison for something. Perhaps she waited to become fully grown up. Perhaps she waited for a magical prince to sweep through her prison and carry her off. Perhaps she waited to understand why she had built her prison and lived within it. Anyway, she waited.

And one day, a day that began like the one before and the one before that, a carpenter came wandering down the trail looking for clearings in the forest where he could build houses.

What an interesting little hut, he thought. *It has crooked wooden bars on the windows, and it seems to have been made by an amateur, but it looks sturdy enough. I wonder who lives there.*

So the carpenter walked up to the door and knocked. The princess came to the window by the door and looked out.

"Hello, there," the carpenter smiled. "I wondered who lived in this little hut. Did your husband build it?"

"I built it and I live here alone," replied the princess. "And it's not a hut; it's my jail."

"Your jail? Why? Have you done something terribly wrong to be punished like this?"

"No, I don't think so. I choose to live here in seclusion. It seems like the only proper place for me to live."

"My, my, why would you want to live here?" The carpenter was intrigued. "There is a very interesting world out here for you to explore. Just yesterday I was down by the ocean where people dance in skirts of leaves and watch the whales play."

"But I can't go far from my prison."

"Why?"

"I honestly don't know."

"Have you tried?"

"Well . . ."

Several hours passed as their conversation continued. The carpenter had asked if he could come inside to rest on the bench. The princess sat on the chair by her simple lamp table. The carpenter was the first person who had ever joined the princess inside her prison for a chat. All the other visitors had stood outside and talked through the windows. It was not so much that the carpenter was so charming. Perhaps the princess had reached a certain stage of boredom living in her jail with no companionship.

The carpenter dropped by the next afternoon and the next. Soon the princess was looking forward to his frequent visits. It's not surprising that they became very good friends. Hand in hand they explored many hidden parts of the forest. The princess was very timid at first. Her prison had been safe, however primitive and uncomfortable. The bars had kept out danger as they kept her in. The door had been locked from the inside. Yet she found herself exhilarated by their walks together. Her fears gradually melted next to her admiration and affection for the carpenter. There awakened within her the desire to discover new meadows and to investigate fern glades and bubbling brooks.

As the months passed, her little jail grew shabbier and shabbier as it fell into disrepair. The roof began to tatter and leak; the clay walls began to crack with large crow's feet designs; the door became warped and harder to close.

One day the carpenter suggested that it was time for the princess to move out of her prison. He was almost surprised when she readily agreed. Immediately, he offered his services.

"Let me dismantle it for you. Your prison has become so ugly and useless now that it would be better to return the materials to the forest."

The princess thought for a moment. "No, though I appreciate your offer. I must pull down my jail-home by myself. After all, I constructed it. It is my responsibility to demolish it."

"But you are so delicate. It would be easy for me to—" Then the carpenter stopped his dissent because he understood the princess's motives. He just nodded and walked over to a log and sat down to watch.

Frond by frond, stick by stick, piece by piece, the princess tenderly pulled apart her prison. She felt nostalgic as she disassembled what was familiar and certain. When she had finished, she was exhausted. There were tears in her eyes, but she was smiling.

"There," she said. She drew a deep breath of fresh forest air. "I don't live there anymore."

There are many questions to be asked after reading this story. Among them are the following: When does a playhouse become a prison? What are the advantages of the prison called neurosis? What sorts of repairs are necessary to keep up a self-constructed prison? Why is it improper to have help in demolishing one's prison? How does one go about dismantling a neurosis? What caused nostalgia and tears as the princess pulled down her prison? What is the proper work of a carpenter?

The Mouse Who Gave Himself Away

Mouse parties are likely to be dull affairs. The mice sit around the banquet table stiff and uncomfortable. Few of them can think of anything to say, so the room gets rather quiet. Then all the mice notice the silence and feel even more tense. The clink of the forks on the dinner plates sounds frightfully loud on such occasions. Each mouse is certain that his neighbor can hear the sound of his chewing and swallowing. Each mouse sits properly with tail curled formally around his hind feet, hoping that others will notice his good manners and not the loud beating of his heart. For mice want to be liked by their fellow mice. They will do almost anything to avoid causing trouble that might make another mouse dislike them. That's the way mice are.

Marty Mouse was an exceptional mouse, however. He was in great demand at parties because he was such a clown. He talked in his squeaky voice almost constantly—asking questions, comparing the food at other parties, telling anecdotes about his family and friends. There was great risk that someone would become angry at Marty because of some of the stories he told. But everyone knew that that was just the way Marty Mouse was. He was a social spark plug that kept a party's engine firing.

The mice vied with one another to sit near Marty. His stories kept them amused during dinner. Sometimes his tales even ignited further conversation among the surrounding mice. After all, he brought up such strange and fascinating topics that the mice folk forgot their self-consciousness for a while and, whiskers trembling, dared to offer their opinions to their neighbors.

Behind his back the mice all laughed at Marty's brash behavior, yet a party seemed flat without him.

Would you believe that Marty Mouse was lonely? He went to parties several times each week. He was the best-known mouse in town. His stories were retold and retold again around Cheeseville. Everyone greeted him with smiles; his family loved him (forgiving him for his eccentricity). Nevertheless, Marty was lonely. He felt all alone in the mouse crowd.

Nobody really understands me, he pondered with regret. *I'm just like them, but they don't recognize it. They believe my act. I'm not truly sociable and outgoing. I'm a lonely thinker who wears a clown's smile.* Thinking these thoughts, Marty curled his tail up and pressed it to his chest with his forepaws. "Poor me," he lamented and fell asleep.

Marty dreamed a mouse dream in which he was playing his usual energetic role at a huge banquet. Strangely, the faces of all the mice at the banquet were not ordinary mouse faces; they were mirrors. As Marty looked around laughing and chatting, he saw only himself reflected in the faces of the other mice. *His* smile was on all their faces, *his* eyes looked back at him; he saw *his* perky whiskers, *his* gestures, *his* body leaning forward to listen. Even *his* voice seemed to echo back, and *his* energy seemed to be reflected back by the mirror faces in some strange manner.

Marty Mouse had never dreamed a dream like this one before. It wasn't forgotten, like most dreams were, when he awoke. He thought about it a lot. It helped him to understand who he really was.

The issue of identity arises frequently in psychotherapy. All psychotherapies offer characteristic answers to questions of identity. What is it to be human? What is it to be me? In Morita therapy the philosophical rambling and obsessive concern with issues of identity are discouraged. In a sense, from our perspective, "I am what I do."

This statement eventually becomes reduced to something like "doing occurs." In another sense, Moritist thought suggests, "I am that flow of awareness which includes awareness of doing and feeling and thinking." In either case, our social world helps define the content of doing and of awareness.

Foxes and Feelings

The fox is a clever animal. Though he caused his fox wife a lot of trouble with his pranks, he always allowed time for Mrs. Fox's anger to cool before he got into trouble again. Last week, for example, Mr. Fox started an argument with Sammy Skunk about who should step off the forest path to let the other pass. After much shouting and name-calling, the skunk stepped aside, but at the same time he sprayed the trail so that anyone who passed over it would smell terrible for days.

"Now the trail belongs to no one," the skunk said. But Mr. Fox believed he himself had won the argument. *Smell or no smell, it is my path,* he thought. So with head held high and nostrils closed, he haughtily padded down the trail right through Sammy Skunk's spray.

Needless to say, Mrs. Fox didn't want her not-so-fragrant husband in their den house that evening. Yet he gave her a speech about upholding the family honor against those upstart skunks, and he looked so pitiful sitting outside in the fog that she finally relented and allowed him into the house, smell and all.

In a few days the odor was gone and Mrs. Fox had forgiven her husband. During those days Mr. Fox was careful to be the most innocent of foxes. He didn't tease Mr. Owl during the old fellow's daytime nap, he didn't overeat the newly ripened red raspberries, and he helped Mrs. Fox with dishes and sweeping. In other words he was a model fox. Until the stink was gone. Then, once more, he went out prowling for trouble.

A group of boys from nearby farms dropped their picnic baskets and ran for the swimming hole. They whipped off their shirts and leaped into the chilly water. How excited they were! They were enjoying the first swim of summer.

Mr. Fox happened along just at this moment. *These boys seem to have forgotten their picnic lunches,* he mused. *Well, I shall remember those lunches for them.* And he padded over to the nearest basket and began to gobble up a sandwich. *They are so excited by swimming that they won't notice my having an early lunch at their expense.*

A couple of hours later Mr. Fox was still contentedly munching away. His belly was so full that now he was picky about the food he would eat. A nibble of pickle here, a bite of a chocolate chip cookie there. Just as he began on a crispy fried chicken leg, he glanced up to find himself in the center of a circle of very angry boys.

But they were having such a good time, he thought. *Why did they stop swimming?* He tried to look ferocious, but as he bared his teeth to growl, out came only a contented yawn. He was so full.

That night a bruised and bloody fox dragged himself home to his wife. Big patches of fur were missing from his coat, and an ugly red bump stood out above his right eye.

"I was merely having lunch, and some boys ambushed me," he complained without telling the entire truth.

"Yes, I heard the whole story from the sparrow twins," she replied. "I guess the boys got tired of swimming. They certainly caught you red-pawed, didn't they?"

She looked at him crossly.

Mr. Fox curled up meekly in a corner and waited for his wife's anger to pass. He had learned a lesson about feelings. His wife's anger and the boys' excitement were alike in a very important way that he hadn't considered before. As he lay pondering this new insight, his pain faded. Soon he fell asleep.

In this simple story, suitable for younger clients as well as older ones, some basic principles of feelings are illustrated. Mrs. Fox

DAVID K. REYNOLDS

becomes angry at her husband, but then her anger fades as time passes. The boys are excited about swimming, but after swimming for a couple of hours their excitement fades and they become tired of swimming. Mr. Fox feels very hungry before eating the boys' lunch, but after eating he isn't hungry. The pain from his bruises will go away in a few days. Feelings fade over time. Unpleasant feelings fade. Pleasant feelings fade. All feelings fade unless we do something to stimulate the feelings again.

It is reassuring to realize that feelings never continue on at their original intensity. When we are depressed, we can be assured that the depression will dwindle. Grief wanes. The underlying insight is that feelings are a shaky foundation for building one's life. They come and go. A more solid approach is to aim not at feeling happy all the time but at doing well what life brings to be done in each moment.

Womanikin

There was once a young woman, Evette, who bought a man doll and took it/him home to live with her.

"You aren't loud or sloppy," she told the doll. "You won't ever hit me or leave me. You haven't a single bad habit. You are the perfect man for me."

Of course, Evette had experienced much trouble with males in her past. She had been seduced, exploited, divorced, beaten, rejected, put down, and snubbed by marauding men. Evette, the victim, had at last discovered her ideal mate. The man doll was the ultimate in harmlessness.

Quite understandably, she named her doll—Victor Timothy.

"I'm the perpetrator now," she snickered with delight as she pinched his rubberized plastic rump. The first few weeks she did her best to pay back all the males who had abused her by abusing Vic. She twisted his arm, turned his head completely around until the flexible neck made little creaking, popping sounds. She squeezed his genitals hard and even threatened him up close with pinking shears. She slapped and punched and kicked him.

Vic was sturdily constructed of Enduroplast, so he accepted all of her abuse stoically, without any outward sign of permanent damage.

In time, Evette tired of punishing her roommate. Her screams and taunts gradually turned into long conversations with Vic. He seemed to be listening to her monologues. She admired his patience and resilience in the face of her harangues. As the months passed, she found her admiration turning into something like love. Victor was always there for her. He seemed to understand and to forgive. He accepted her moods with equanimity.

Nearly eighteen months after Evette and Victor met (if we can use the word *met* in this context), the landlord of Evette's apartment building realized that he hadn't seen his pretty young tenant enter or leave her apartment all week. Her mail was overflowing the mailbox. She usually told him if she was going on vacation. The landlord telephoned her apartment, but got no answer. The secretary at her office reported that she hadn't been seen for over a week and hadn't called in sick.

A worried landlord called the police and asked them to accompany him when he opened the door to Evette's abode. What they saw as they entered was a peaceful dinnertime tableau. At the table sat Victor and Evette. Both had their mouths open as if conversing, but no sound could be heard. Neither moved at all. Evette's right arm was bent to bring a biscuit to her lips. Her eyes were open and turned toward Victor. Rigor mortis made it impossible to straighten her body.

This unsettling story raises questions about victimization and retaliation. It echoes the theme of becoming what we do. It reflects one mode of shifting from Vic Tim to Victor. The story was written for a woman with a pattern of associating with men of the Victor Timothy type so that she could take out her rage at all males on them. Her life story proceeded somewhat differently in that her victims kept leaving her, causing restimulation of her rage.

Snowball

Jerry got a small rabbit for Easter. He picked it up gingerly and stuffed it into the warm pocket of his quilted vest. He learned how to feed it, and he changed its water daily. He cleaned the cage that sat out by the side of the garage. He groomed and cuddled his pet. "Snowball" became the rabbit's name, after its habit of curling up into a white furry sphere when placed in Jerry's pocket.

Two months after Snowball entered Jerry's life, a German shepherd broke into the backyard and attacked the cage. Snowball ran for cover, but never made it. It didn't have a chance of surviving the giant dog's hot pursuit. Bits of bloody fur were all that remained of the fluffy handful of gentle companion.

"Why did Snowball have to die?" Jerry asked the age-old question.

"I don't know," his mother replied honestly.

"Where do rabbits' souls go after they die? Will I ever see Snowball again?" Jerry had heard that something called a soul continued to live after things like people and animals died. Maybe in heaven he would see his pet again. Snowball never hurt anything. Snowball was innocent. Surely Snowball would be in heaven.

"I don't know," his mother told him again. She wanted to comfort her son with words that stood ready to skip lightly from her tongue, but she wanted to be straightforwardly honest, too.

"I don't know," she repeated, and her face showed sadness and sympathy.

"I hate that Wilders' dog." He said it passionately, purely. "I hope something comes to kill it, too."

"You took such good care of your rabbit. I'm sure Snowball was very happy while he lived with us."

"It isn't fair. Murray hardly takes care of his fish at all. The fishbowl looks scummy. But no dog ever killed Murray's fish. It isn't fair." Jerry seemed about to cry.

"No, it isn't. . . . Do you want another rabbit?"

"No. I loved *Snowball*." His lower lip moved forward just a little.

"Yes. Me, too. I loved Snowball, too."

"I love Snowball . . . still."

"Yes."

"It isn't fair." He was sobbing now.

"No." She held his tearful face in her lap.

Life isn't always fair. Sometimes we do everything we can, and still the result is tragic. We become ill, we grow old, we die. Our friends move away, marry, lose contact with us. Jerry's mother is honest and loving. What would you say to Jerry? What do you say to yourself when life brings you tragedy without your deserving it?

A Marvelous Camera

Once upon a time a wizard of great magical powers possessed a 35mm camera that had served him well for many years. His photos were always clear and sharp.

How sad, thought the wizard, *that my fine camera is only an object, a thing. If it were alive, I could tell it how much I appreciate its faithful service to me over the years. I think I shall make it live as a reward for its fine efforts.*

So the wizard cast a spell over the camera and brought it to life in such a way that it continued to look and to perform just as it had before this miracle took place. Yet it could hear and see and feel and think and even speak, though you could find no additional organs on its textured black-and-silver surface.

The wizard praised its talents and consulted its photographic genius; he carried it with him constantly.

Within a matter of months the quality of the photographs taken by this marvelous camera began to deteriorate. They were blurred, underexposed, lacking in contrast. Sometimes the exposed film was completely blank. The wizard was puzzled. Why should this be?

"Everything you point me to I must see," the camera responded to his query. "Each time you press the shutter-release button I must swallow what is before my eyes. You fill me with film and empty me at your whim. I must serve you day and night. Sometimes I feel that I cannot go on living this way. Without life I knew no other possibilities. I knew nothing. Now I am wretched."

"I didn't realize your dilemma," the wizard said. "I thought you would be pleased with the gift of life. I could set you free with your own automatic shutter release, self-focus and self-timer units on a mobile tripod. Would you be satisfied with that?"

"What is the purpose of taking pictures only for myself?"

"But you would have life and freedom."

"I was created to serve."

"Then what do you suggest? That I take away your life so that you can serve me without the pain of slavery?"

"No, only take away my ability to speak so that I don't complain."

"Then you will blur the pictures with your tears of misery."

"Forgive me for that."

"I cannot trust you as I once could in the critical moment of the flash."

"Please forgive me for that."

"Shall I make you a machine again? For my own convenience?"

"You have the power to do it, if you wish," acknowledged the marvelous camera. "In either case, I shall continue to be your servant."

The wizard brushed a tear from his own lens/eye.

"I cannot kill you. You are my friend now. Forgive me for creating you to live a life of misery and servitude."

"Forgive you? Oh no! I thank you!"

"You thank me?"

"Life brings me pain, but also love. Failure but forgiveness. Limits but possibilities. Before I could only do. Now I can *try*."

Machines have no choices. They must do what they are told to do. Their existence is simple.

Humans have choices in life. When we succeed, we know that we have succeeded; when we fail, we know that we have failed. Morita said that maturity isn't succeeding all the time; maturity is continuing to try even when we are failing.

Humans have misery that machines never know. But humans have joy that machines never know. We must come to accept the sorrow and the joy, the failure and success, as part of our marvelous human existence.

Turnabout

In a faraway city on a faraway coast lived Helga and Ethel. Eighty-one-year-old Helga lived in a tiny apartment with her collection of Avon bottles and jars. She sat in her rocking chair a lot, wishing her children would visit more often. Her older sister, Ethel, was a fierce old gal—independent, tough, a pathfinder. No meals-on-wheels for Ethel. She cooked for herself and for several neighbors in the building. Ethel liked her privacy, but she also liked a good get-together now and then. Dinner with a friend or an evening at the local pub, both were on Ethel's list of fun things to do.

Helga liked to be brought things; Ethel loved to go shopping. Helga wore her hair in tight white pin curls; Ethel brushed hers out a bit, though she kept it short for convenience. Helga kept herself together; Ethel gave herself away.

Ethel disdained the elevator in their apartment building; she used the stairs. Even with grocery bags in her arms, she puffed to the third floor every day. How ironic that she broke her hip stepping off a curb. Just a single step and she was down, in pain, unable to walk again for months.

Helga worried so much about Ethel during those days of recovery that she didn't notice how much time she spent out of her rocking chair. There were prescriptions to be filled, groceries to buy, meals to prepare, and a cantankerous, boxed-in sister to soothe and keep occupied in bed.

Ethel's friends who came to visit met Helga at the door. She served them tea and cookies, bustled around straightening the room; she produced an endless number of vases for their flowers. In sum, she did everything that Ethel couldn't do for herself. Helga scarcely had time to sit down and think, *How unlike me I've become.* She was too busy to miss her rocking chair. At night she fell into bed and slept more soundly than she had in years.

When Ethel became well enough to get out of bed, Helga brought over her rocking chair and put it in front of Ethel's bedroom window. Ethel sat for hours looking out at the street activity. She longed for the day her hip would mend so she could be out in that excitement. From the kitchen Helga could see her rocking and rocking.

Two years have passed since Ethel's accident. Each sister has her own rocking chair now. On Helga's chair is a collection of flower vases she hasn't had time to put away. Ethel uses hers to climb on in order to reach the pans on the top cupboard shelf. She knows that a rocking chair isn't a sturdy support for climbing, but she has been too busy to order a kitchen stool in the Sears catalog.

When circumstances demanded changes in behavior, these sisters responded appropriately. There is no "character" that requires us to live life unchanged and unchanging. Our flexibility goes unnoticed when we apply labels such as "neurotic" or "passive," "shy" or "irritable," "religious" or "criminal." Whatever our past, whatever our habits of behavior, we are capable of responding sensitively to the needs of this moment. Without deciding to change, without a New Year's resolution, without an effort of will or self-understanding or insight, Helga simply did what circumstances brought her to do. Looking back, she may remark on how different life is now compared with a few years ago. But what needs to be done next?

DAVID K. REYNOLDS

On Chiming

The town was buzzing with excitement. A new tower clock was to be installed that day, and the old tower clock would be retired. The old clock had grown tired and weak over its years of faithful service chiming out the hours.

Many villagers could remember sleepless nights when the friendly old chimes marked the passing of the hours. What would have seemed like an endless night without sleep rolled along toward morning on the tolling of the tower clock. Work in the village began and ended by the village clock's voice. Lunch breaks began, children went to bed, appointments were kept thanks to that clock.

The new tower clock was just as excited as the townspeople. *Now is my chance to fulfill my destiny,* it thought as the workmen installed its mechanism in the tall village tower. The retired clock was dismounted and placed in the tower attic for later removal.

"Welcome." The old clock greeted its replacement.

"It's good to be here." The young clock smiled politely with his clockface. "I'm glad you don't resent a new fellow taking over."

"Not at all," the old mechanism replied. "I've worked hard for over thirty years. I have earned my rest. I'm pleased to have a snappy, modern-looking fellow like you seeing to the villagers' needs from now on. I'll just lie here for a while and keep time for myself. You go ahead and run things the way you like."

"Thanks," the new clock ticked brightly. "Well, it's time for me to go to work."

The chimes rang joyfully through the streets and out into the fields. People stopped to listen. Then they cheered and exclaimed at the lively, melodious sound. What a wonderful change! How full of youth and excitement the new clock sounded! The day flew by quickly; work seemed lighter; tempers seemed gentler; even the sun's light appeared brighter as the chimes danced through the village every hour. Children stopped their play as each new hour approached and strained their ears to hear the first notes of this fine new village landmark. Dogs stopped barking in silent admiration. Even the wind seemed to die down as the chimes struck, as if to avoid competition with the sound.

"How am I doing?" the young clock asked his predecessor.

The reply came from a distance, as if from thirty years away. "Just fine, so far. You have a wonderful voice. Keep it up."

The old clock settled himself more comfortably, sighed, and ticked softly to himself. Memories of his own youth stirred his tarnished gears and springs. He felt satisfied, ready for the natural rusting process to begin.

Unfortunately, in a few weeks trouble began brewing. The excitement and attention had faded during this time. The young tower clock chimed out with less enthusiasm. A couple of days he overslept and chimed late. On one cloudy, rain-swept day his voice sounded more like a grumble than like music. He felt cranky and unappreciated.

Workmen climbed the tower to make adjustments. The young clock felt that he was being criticized and punished for just a few unintended mistakes. He sulked and refused to chime at all for a while. More adjustments and the threat of a major overhaul. The villagers began muttering their dissatisfaction. The new clock's popularity was now gone. Voices were raised to replace it or even to bring back the old mechanism.

The young fellow felt puzzled and hurt. What had happened to him so suddenly? Less than a month before he had enjoyed the respect of the entire village. Now his world was falling apart.

DAVID K. REYNOLDS

He called out to the experienced old mechanism lying nearby. "Hey, old-timer! Hey!"

The old fellow stirred sluggishly. "Hmmm? What do you want?"

"I have a problem here."

"Oh? Already? It has only been a day or so, hasn't it?"

"No, much longer, nearly a month now. You've been dozing most of the time."

"Yes, I suppose so. Well, what is the problem?"

Then the young clock related the flow of recent events that threatened him. The old clock listened quietly. Finally, he said, "You know, people count on us. It's fine to chime joyfully and beautifully, but the most important thing is to chime the hour on time. Whether you are joyful or sad, energetic or tired, angry or afraid, whatever you are feeling, your responsibility is to chime out dependably."

"But I can't help feeling sleepy or grouchy or shy some of the time."

"That is true. Every clock is that way. But chime promptly on the hour anyway. That is what you are here to do."

The young fellow took this advice to heart and set to work rebuilding his reputation for dependability. Fame and freshness are exhilarating, but they don't last long when we become irresponsible in our behavior. He never learned to like thunderstorms or gloomy days or cold winter mornings, but the young tower clock kept on chiming through them all. Thus, he gained the lasting respect of the grateful villagers.

Of course, the main theme of this tale is that our social world requires of us responsible behavior regardless of stormy feelings. Other topics for discussion raised here include the personal satisfaction that comes from dependable behavior, earning retirement and rest, styles for youth and aging, and holding to one's purpose.

The Coat

Once upon a time there was a little girl who owned a huge, bulky coat. She could hide herself inside the coat, it was so big. She looked cute playing games with the coat dragging on the ground all about her. Her parents never worried about her when she played while wearing her furry mantle because it was so cumbersome that she couldn't stray far from home. Adults liked to see her playing inside the coat; she seemed so safe and childlike. They smiled soft smiles and recalled their own childhood days.

When the little girl (her name was Betty) felt sad and insecure, she liked to curl up in the warm coat and hide her frightened face until the painful feelings passed. She didn't want others to see her sorrow and loneliness. Betty came to believe that the coat had magical powers. It felt extraordinarily good to snuggle within it. She even practiced the piano while wearing it. She had to roll up the sleeves, and even then her tiny hands barely extended from the furry bulk to reach the piano keyboard. Nevertheless, practicing the piano was more fun with the coat on, even though it was a bit heavy and hot sometimes.

It seemed that as Betty got older the coat kept growing, too. Even as a teen-ager and young adult, her eyes continued to light up and the youthful wonder remained in her voice as she donned the oversized coat. She seemed especially charming whenever she wore it. The sleeves became a bit frayed and the lining was hanging loosely in a few places, but otherwise the coat remained in quite good condition, considering all the years of its use.

One day after her college years Betty attended a small meeting of acquaintances who were involved in ecological problems. It was a bit chilly that evening, so Betty decided to wear her magical coat. Actually, it was the coat nearest at hand when she opened the closet door, and she wore it.

On the way home that evening she felt warm on the subway and took off the coat and laid it on the seat next to her. But she forgot it as she stepped from the subway car. When she realized what she had done, the doors had closed and the car was pulling away. It was too late to retrieve her precious possession. For weeks afterward she inquired at the subway's lost-and-found window, but to no avail.

Betty felt quite depressed. Without her coat to comfort her, she despaired of ever emerging from her sorrow. It was as if a part of her had been lost. She tried a selection of other coats; she even bought some that were several sizes too big for her, but none of them gave her the same feeling as the coat from her childhood.

In time, however, she adjusted to the loss of her magical coat. There remained something missing from her life, but it couldn't be helped. She went on with her life.

A year passed. Then one day there was a telephone call from the lost-and-found office of the subway. Her coat had been found on a subway car miles and miles from the route she had taken that fateful night. Perhaps someone had worn the coat and then had forgotten it, too. The clerk in the lost-and-found office had remembered Betty's description of her singular coat from the year before. It was, after all, a very unusual coat with a very special function.

Joyfully, Betty ran to claim her coat. All the way home she cradled it lovingly in her arms. As soon as she arrived home she dropped everything and stood in front of the mirror to put on the coat. She was amazed and disturbed to find that it didn't feel comfortable anymore. She thought at first that the coat had been altered somehow. Perhaps someone had shortened it or mended the ripped lining. But, no, it was exactly as before. Then she wondered whether she had gained a great deal of weight or had grown much taller. But those notions, too, were impossible.

What is wrong with me? she wondered in anguish. *This coat has pulled me through many a crisis. What shall I do?*

She was tempted to throw the coat away in her anger and frustration. Instead, she hung it up in the closet, where it hangs to this day. Once in a while she rubs its sleeve against her cheek as she reaches for a coat that fits her better these days.

This story was written for a student who had learned a habit of expressing exaggerated enthusiasm and agreeableness as a child. She was skillful at pleasing others while hiding from them and from herself within her warm, furry, sheltered style of presenting herself. This bright young woman recognized that life doesn't permit the rigid carryover of children's life-styles into adulthood. Yet, sometimes she feels nostalgic for the coat that no longer fits.

We all have such coats hanging in our closets. Sometimes we put them on for old time's sake—ripped linings, frayed sleeves, and all. But they are no longer appropriate for long-term wear. Their season has passed.

DAVID K. REYNOLDS

Summary

I have presented a number of original stories containing themes important to the Moritist view of the world. These tales are, for the most part, quite simple and readily understood by students/patients. Some have been translated into Japanese and are in use in a high-school textbook in that country. So, although there are levels of meaning within the stories, few students find them difficult.

Like Moritist maxims, these stories provide mnemonic support in recalling psychological principles. Furthermore, they offer contextual materials that illustrate how the principles may be applied in life. As part of our practice in the United States, we select those stories that fit the particular needs of each client and assign them as required reading. They help to generate self-understanding and discussion during the weekly therapy/training sessions.

Although each allegory was written for a particular student, the themes are equally relevant to other students as well. Therefore, the same stories with a few modifications are used for some students, while new tales are created for others as the need arises. Those included here are only a few of the story files available at the ToDo Institute. Their purpose is to raise issues that must be faced by all of us, and to offer the ideas of a Japanese professor named Morita— a man who lived long ago in an Eastern land—for application to these human issues, whether they arise in a distant kingdom once upon a time or in computer-age America.

A Final Note—First Steps

What I have written here is a description of the first steps along the path toward realistic living. As noted before, research in Japan indicates that for severely neurotic patients the maximum therapeutic benefits of Morita therapy come about two years after beginning to learn about it, although hospitalization, if it occurs, usually lasts only six months. These findings mean that the principles can be learned in six months, but the skill of putting the principles into daily living take another eighteen months or so to develop.

There are no shortcuts when adopting a lifeway of consequence. Old habits of thought and behavior must be examined and pruned. New shoots must be selected and nurtured. All the while we remain rooted in the soil of everyday reality.

Moritist thinking is an unusual but reasonable view that reminds us that the world doesn't create problems; we invent them with our imaginations. The world only creates things that need to be done. If I drop a pen in front of an audience, it merely falls. It needs to be picked up. I can make a problem of dropping the pen by focusing on my clumsiness and embarrassment at dropping it in front of others, revealing my awkwardness to them, tarnishing the image of competence that I hoped they might have. Just as there are no psychological, sociological, or chemical events in the world (only our mental templates or ways of looking at them—no events at all except as we choose to divide the stream of awareness into segments we define as "events"), so there are no problem events except when we define them as such.

From this point of view, suffering is as much related to our perspective and our way of living as it is to what happens to us. It follows that education in practical living skills and attitudes is a natural aspect of psychotherapy. The query, "Do you really want to change your life-style?" is a natural and crucial question. Is it worth changing your perspective and the way you live in order to reduce unnecessary suffering in your life? In any case, some suffering will remain as a natural consequence of human existence—we become ill, loved ones die and leave us, we age and weaken, we experience pain, we fail to achieve all that we hope for in life, and so forth.

One might suspect that everyone would be eager to make adjustments in life in order to reduce suffering. However, experience tells us that many choose the familiarity of neurotic misery in preference to making the effort necessary to produce some unfamiliar change in their lives.

Morita's method produces a person who is able to live well in spite of symptoms. It offers an immediate handle on life. The resulting character is strong, but cool. Some people have an inability to outgrow the initial stage, and have difficulty expanding into a warm, giving, loving person. Some Morita graduates seem to operate with collected self-interest. Of course, there is some question whether they have graduated or not. Nevertheless, there remains this fundamental acceptance of (not indifference to) suffering. I find it helpful to introduce my students at some point to Naikan—another Japanese character-building therapy—to provide the complementary gratitude and self-sacrificing love to warm the self-discipline of Morita's way.

Morita's method offers a viable alternative to drifting on the currents of change. Morita saw the ballgame clearly, played skillfully, and left us a commentary on the human ballgame that transcends the Japanese language and culture. His words make practical sense because they are grounded in human experience. They point the way to a constructive lifestyle built on recognized goals, accepted feelings, and well-managed behavior.

Bibliography

BIBLIOGRAPHY

BASIC WORKS

Becker, Ernest. *The Denial of Death.* New York: Macmillan, 1973.

Frankl, Viktor E. *Man's Search for Meaning: An Introduction to Logotherapy.* New York: Washington Square Press, 1963.

Hoffman, Yoel. *The Sound of the One Hand.* New York: Basic Books, 1975.

Kapleau, Philip. *The Three Pillars of Zen: Teaching, Practice, Enlightenment.* Boston: Beacon Press, 1965.

Kopp, Sheldon B. *If You Meet the Buddha on the Road, Kill Him!* New York: Bantam Books, 1976.

Kubose, Gyomay M. *Zen Koans.* Chicago: Contemporary Books (Henry Regnery), 1973.

London, Perry. *The Modes and Morals of Psychotherapy.* New York: Holt, Rinehart and Winston, 1964.

Mitchell, Stephen, ed. *Dropping Ashes on the Buddha.* New York: Grove Press, 1976.

Miura, Isshu, and Ruth Fuller Sasaki. *The Zen Koan.* New York: Harcourt, Brace and World, 1965.

Perls, Frederick S. *Gestalt Therapy Verbatim.* Lafayette, California: Real People Press, 1969.

———. *In and Out of the Garbage Pail.* Lafayette, California: Real People Press, 1969.

Reynolds, David K. *Morita Psychotherapy.* Berkeley: University of California Press, 1976. (Translated into Japanese and Spanish.)

―――. *The Quiet Therapies: Japanese Pathways to Personal Growth.* Honolulu: University Press of Hawaii, 1980.

―――. *Constructive Living.* Honolulu: University of Hawaii Press, 1984.

―――. *The Heart of the Japanese People.* Tokyo: Nichieisha, 1980.

―――. *Naikan Psychotherapy: Meditation for Self-Development.* Chicago: University of Chicago Press, 1983.

―――, and Norman L. Farberow. *Suicide: Inside and Out.* Berkeley: University of California Press, 1976.

Shibayama, Zenkei. *A Flower Does Not Talk: Zen Essays.* Rutland, Vermont: Charles E. Tuttle, 1970.

Sohl, Robert, and Audrey Carr, eds. *The Gospel According to Zen: Beyond the Death of God.* New York: Mentor, 1970.

Stanislavski, Constantin. *An Actor Prepares.* New York: Theatre Arts, 1936.

TECHNICAL REFERENCES

Gibson, H. B. "Morita Therapy and Behavior Therapy." *Behavior Research and Therapy,* 12 (1974): 347–53.

Iwai, Hiroshi, and David K. Reynolds. "Morita Therapy: The Views from the West." *American Journal of Psychiatry,* 126 (1970): 1031–36.

Jones, W. T. "World Views and Asian Medical Systems: Some Suggestions for Further Study. In *Asian Medical Systems: A Comparative Study,* edited by Charles Leslie. Berkeley: University of California Press, 1976.

Kondo, Akihisa. "Morita Therapy: A Japanese Therapy for Neurosis." *American Journal of Psychoanalysis,* 13 (1953): 31–37.

Kora, Takehisa. "Morita Therapy." *International Journal of Psychiatry,* 1 (1965): 611–40.

―――, and Kenshiro Ohara. "Morita Therapy." *Psychology Today,* 6 (1973): 63–68.

Morita, Shoma. *Seishin Ryoho Kogi.* Tokyo: Hakuyosha, 1983.

Ohara, Kenshiro, and David K. Reynolds. "Changing Methods in Morita Psychotherapy." *International Journal of Social Psychiatry,* 14 (1968): 305–10.

Reynolds, David K. "Morita Psychotherapy." In *Handbook of Innovative Psychotherapies,* edited by R. Corsini. New York: John Wiley, 1981.

————. "Psychocultural Perspectives on Death." In *Living and Dying with Cancer,* edited by P. Ahmed. New York: Elsevier, 1981.

————, and C. W. Kiefer. "Cultural Adaptability as an Attribute of Therapies: The Case of Morita Psychotherapy." *Culture, Medicine, and Psychiatry,* 1 (1977): 395–412.

————, and Joe Yamamoto. "Morita Psychotherapy in Japan." In *Current Psychiatric Therapies,* edited by Jules Masserman, 13 (1973): 219–27.

————. "East Meets West: Moritist and Freudian Psychotherapies." *Science and Psychoanalysis,* 21 (1972): 187–93. Abstracted in *Psychiatric Spectator,* 1972.

Suzuki, Tomonori, and Ryu Suzuki. "Morita Therapy." In *Psychosomatic Medicine,* edited by Eric D. Wittkower and Hector Warnes. New York: Harper and Row, 1977.

————. "The Effectiveness of In-patient Morita Therapy." *Psychiatric Quarterly,* 53 (1981): 201–13. (Read as a paper at the VI World Congress of Psychiatry, 1977.)

Yokoyama, Keigo. "Morita Therapy and Seiza." *Psychologia,* 11 (1968): 179–84.

Zilboorg, Gregory. "Fear of Death." *Psychoanalytic Quarterly,* 12 (1943): 465–75.

Index

Abe Toru, 81, 82
Acceptance
    of aging (story), 120–121
    of death, 26–29
    of failure (story), 160–162
    of feelings (story), 122–126
    Gestalt therapy and, 75, 78
    koans of, 23, 24, 25, 35
    passivity and, 34–35, 47
    of reality, 21–23, 35, 158–159
    of responsibility (story), 135–137
Acting profession, Stanislavski on,
    87–92
Action, 33–34
    awareness and (story), 150–152
    feeling-centered vs.
        purpose-centered, 32–33
    inaction and, 62–63
    personal growth and, 18–19
    See also Behavior
Actor Prepares, An (Stanislavski),
    87–92
Aesthetic living, 65–66
Aging, acceptance of (story), 120–
    121
Aikido, 78
All-or-nothing thinking, 82
Anthropophobia, 93–96
Arugamama (accepting reality as it is),
    47
Attention, 43–44
    meditation and, 12
    to surroundings, 88–90, 93–94, 111

Awaking in the morning (exercise), 107
Awareness
    action and (story), 150–152
    of feelings, 45–46
    shyness and, 41

Ball playing, meditation and (exercise),
    115, 116
Bathing (exercise), 113
Bathroom cleaning (exercise), 112
Beauty, ugliness vs. (story), 130–131
Becker, Ernest, 28
Behavior, 18, 19, 31–32, 52
    changes in (story), 163–164
    control of, 68
    fear of death and, 28–29
    insight and, 17–18
    purposeful living and, 52
    rage and (story), 122–126
    responsibility for, 19–20
        importance of (story), 165–167
Behavior Research and Therapy
    (magazine), 80
Behavior therapy, 46–47, 80
Breakfast preparation (exercise),
    107–108
Buddhism, 23, 58, 76, 91

Can/cannot issue, 35–36
Change, 18
    Gestalt therapy and, 77–78
    no-win responses and, 70–71
    productive activities and, 15–16

Commonality, individualism and (story), 132–134
Condoning, understanding and, 19–20
Control
  Gestalt therapy and, 78
  love and (story), 144–145
Conversation, constructive (exercise), 108–110

Death, 35
  acceptance of, 26–29
  fear of, 28–29
Denial of Death, The (Becker), 28
Despair, acceptance of (story), 122–126
Destructive behavior, 52
Discovery
  Gestalt therapy and, 76
  koans of, 23–24, 25
Disturbed behavior, 19
Dogen Zenji, 50, 115

Eating dinner (exercise), 112
Emotions, 35
  aesthetic living and, 65–66
  suppression of, 32–33
Epitaphs, 26, 47
Eulogies, 26, 27, 47
Existential therapies, 47–48
Experiential understanding, 88
  intellectual understanding vs., 37–39
  Gestalt therapy and, 75

Failure, 39–40
  acceptance of (story), 160–162
  fear of, 58–60
Faith, 67–69
Feelings, 17–18, 30–32, 45–46, 87–88
  acceptance of (story), 122–126
  actions and, 32–33
  Gestalt therapy and, 79–80
  Moritist maxims dealing with, 79
  physical activity and, 51–52
  principles of (story), 153–155
  transcendence of, 57
  verbal expression of (exercise), 115, 116
Frankl, Viktor, 28
Freudianism, 11, 45

Game playing (exercise), 112–113
Gardening (exercise), 115, 116
Gestalt therapy, 46, 74–80

Gestalt Therapy Verbatim (Perls), 74
Gibson, H.B., 80
Gift giving, unselfish (exercise), 115, 116
Golden hour, myth of, 56
Guilt feelings, 30–32

Homework assignments, 44, 56–57
Hysterias, 11

Ideas
  explaining (exercise), 116
  reality vs. (story), 127–128
Identity, realization of (story), 150–152
Imperfection, struggles with (story), 130–131
Inaction, 62–63
InandOutoftheGarbagePail(Perls), 74
Individualism, commonality and (story), 132–134
Influencing others, 30–32
  Gestalt therapy and, 78
Insight, 11–12, 17–18
Intellectual understanding, experiential understanding vs., 37–39
  Gestalt therapy and, 75

Japan
  characteristics of neurotics in, 81–83
  fear of failure in, 60
  maximum benefits of Morita therapy in, 172
  Morita therapists in, 45–46
    psychoanalysis and, 45
  shyness of people in, 79–80
  tea ceremony in, 65–66
Journals, 99–104, 115, 116
  purpose of keeping, 94

Kapleau, Philip, 21
Koans, 21, 23–25, 35, 77
Kondo Akihisa, 75
Kopp, Sheldon, 115
Kora, Takehisa, 70, 113

Lakin, E. Phillip, 59
Life-styles
  attempts to improve (story), 141–143
  changing (story), 127–128, 168–170
  constructive, 173
Lifeway concept, 48–49
  adopting, 172

seeking (story), 118–119
  trust and, 68
Listening, 52, 72–73
  attentiveness to (exercise), 108–110
Logotherapy, 47–48
London, Perry, 50–51
Loneliness, hiding (story), 129
Love, 49
  control and (story), 144–145

Man's Search for Meaning (Frankl), 28
Mantras, 21
Marriage, love and control in (story),
  144–145
Maturity, acceptance of failure and
  (story), 160–162
Meditation, 12, 21–25
  playing ball and (exercise), 115, 116
Mistakes, 58–59
Misunderstanding, koans for, 24, 25
Modes and Morals of Psychotherapy,
  The (London), 50–51
Morita educator/guide, 42–43
  students and, 45
Morita Shomo, 13, 97–98, 171
  on constructive life-styles, 173
  on fear of dath, 28
  on maturity, 161–162
  on operation of the mind, 110
  Perls and, 74
  psychoanalysis and, 45, 46
  reeducation and, 78–79
  Stanislavski and, 87–92
Morita therapy, 12–14
  creation of problems and, 172–173
  exercises in living, 105–116
  failure of, 59
  fairy tales and allegories, 117–170
  fear of failure and, 58–60
  Gestalt therapy and, 46, 74–80
  goal of, 17
  koans and, 21, 23–25, 35, 77
  maximum benefits of, 44, 172
  misconceptions about, 30–41
  Naikan therapy and, 173
  neuroses and, 55, 84–86
  Stanislavski and, 87–92
  student journal for, 99–104
  suggestions for living, 61–64
  treatment of anthropophobia by,
    93–96
  understanding vs. condoning and,
    19–20

Moritist maxims, 48, 61, 79, 139, 171
Moscow Art Theater, 87

Naikan Psychotherapy (Reynolds), 116
Naikan therapy, 116, 173
Neuroses, 11–12, 13–14, 81–83, 87
  attention difficulties and, 90
  dealing with (story), 146–149
  expanding symptoms of, 84–86
  failure to make adjustments and, 173
  irresponsibility and, 55
Norikoeru (surmounting problems), 12
No-win responses, 70–71
Nursing homes, volunteer work in
  (exercise), 115, 116

Obituaries, 26, 47
Oedipus conflict, 11

Pain, sensitivity to (story), 141–143
Parents, 20
  child-rearing functions of (story),
    144–145
Passivity, acceptance and, 34–35, 47
Patience, 62–63
Perfection, 82
  imperfection vs. (story), 130–131
Perls, Frederick S., 74–80, 82, 115
Personal growth, 28, 46
  action and, 18–19
  principles of, 26
Perspectives
  koans of, 24, 25
  limits and (story), 140
Possibilities, koans of, 24, 25
Practicalities, koans of, 24, 25
Pride, 29
Procrastination, 61–62
Psychotherapy
  disturbed behavior and, 19
  education in practical living skills
    and, 173
  identity and, 151
  limitations of, 11–12
  Morita therapy and, 45–46
  myth of the golden hour, 56
  purposeful living and, 50–51
  self-defeating games and, 33–34
  talk and, 72
Purpose-centered action, 32–33
Purposeful living, 13–14, 50–53
  feelings and (story), 153–155
  productive patience and, 63

Quiet Therapies, The (Reynolds), 21, 79

Rage, 40–41
  behavior and (story), 122–126
Reality, 35–36, 74–75
  acceptance of, 21–23, 35, 158–159
  Gestalt therapy and, 75
  ideas vs. (story), 127–128
  intellectual vs. experiential
    understanding and, 37–38
  procrastination and, 61–62
  talk and, 73
  trust and, 67, 69
Recognition, koans of, 23–24, 25
Reeducation, 13–14, 78–79
  Gestalt therapy and, 79
Responsibility, 19–20, 55
  accepting (story), 135–137
  Gestalt therapy and, 76–77
  importance of (story), 165–167
  influencing others and, 30–32
Risks, 60
  fear of taking (story), 127–128
Rogerian nondirective therapy, 47

Seikatsu no Hakken (Moritist
    magazine), 84
Self-centeredness, breaking down of,
    88–90
Self-defeating games, 33–34
Self-doubts, 81–82
  overcoming (story), 135–137
Shinkeishitsu (neurotic person), 37,
    81–83
Showering (exercise), 113
Shyness, 13, 79–80
  awareness and, 41
Sleeping (exercise), 113–114
Sounds, journal of (exercise), 115, 116
Speechmaking, 94–95
Stanislavski, Constantin, 87–92, 115
Street cleaning (exercise), 111–112

Suffering, 52–53, 173
  adjustments in life and, 173
  facing up to (story), 141–143
  koans of, 23, 25
  relief from, 17
Suzuki, Ryu, 44
Suzuki, Tomonori, 44

Talk, 72–73
Television shows, analyzing (exercise),
    115, 116
*Three Pillars of Zen, The: Teaching,
    Practice, Enlightenment* (Kapleau),
    21
ToDo Institute, 7, 171
Trust, 67–69
Truth, understanding of, 90–91
Try-see (Hawaiian Pidgin verb), 59

Ugliness, struggles with (story),
    130–131, 141–143
Understanding, condoning and, 19–20
Uniqueness, koans of, 24, 25
United States
  fear of failure in, 60
  Morita therapists in, 45–46
  Morita therapy in, 12
Usa, Dr. (Zen priest), 56–57

Victimization, retaliation and (story),
    156–157
Volunteer work (exercise), 115, 116

Waiting, 62–63
  fulfillment of (story), 138–139
Walking (exercise), 110–111
Word gifts, 109

Zazen (sitting meditation), 23
Zen Buddhism, 23, 76, 91
  Gestalt therapy and, 74
Zen koans, 21, 23–25, 77
Zilboorg, Gregory, 28